A Backdoor to Heaven

Lionel Blue

A Backdoor to Heaven

For sinners who cannot repent; for believers
who never met God and for unbelievers who
have; for all who suffer from spiritual vertigo,
doubt and transcendental *mal-de-mer*; for
those imprisoned in religious systems and
those locked out of them – a reluctant Rabbi
describes how he attempted to break and
enter.

Collins
FOUNT PAPERBACKS

First published in 1979
by Darton, Longman & Todd Ltd, London
This revised edition first published
in 1985 by Fount Paperbacks, London
Third impression June 1986

Made and printed in Great Britain by
William Collins Sons & Co. Ltd, Glasgow

Contents

To whom it may concern

I started to write a book on spirituality as if it were outside me and independent of my own life and experience. It could not be done. It is easy to issue cheques, but what is the capital in the bank? My own experience is poor but it is honest and, though there is not too much of it, I have had to base my life on it and prop up some other people's too. It can stand it.

My life has its holy bits and its profane bits, and I have learnt from both, for there is quite a lot of materialism among the holy and generosity among the profane. I am a reluctant believer, and this story may help those who are "outside" religion and curious, but who are reluctant to join such a strange show. I am also an "insider" – a religious bureaucrat – and it may help other "insiders" who feel that God might be an "outsider" too. It may also help those who suffer from religious indigestion and spiritual *mal-de-mer*.

Truth I learnt in seminaries, honesty I learnt elsewhere. The latter is necessary but not easy, and I thank Kim Holman and Monica Furlong, who encouraged me to write this book, and Dow and Fredzia Marmur, who encouraged me to publish it. I also thank friends in Holland who still help me to see the obvious:

Jaap, Hedda, Rob,

Theo, Marjolein, Jan,

Max, Inez, Beertje

and a friend whose name I forgot or never knew.

In addition to all these friends, slowly I began to suspect I had other teachers, too close for comfort, whom I had never honoured enough or listened to enough. As I wrote a new last chapter for this edition, which brings this quirky pilgrimage up to date, I realized who they were. So I dedicate this last chapter to my own mistakes, the best teachers a man has ever had.

Acknowledgements

The epigraphs to Chapter 1 (Yiddish Riddle Song) and Chapter 23 ("A rabbi fell asleep . . .") are taken from *A Treasury of Jewish Folklore*, edited by Nathan Ausubel. Copyright 1948, 1976, by Crown Publishers Inc. Used by permission of Crown Publishers Inc.

The poem by Zisha Landau (Chapter 4) is translated by Edward Field and is taken from *A Treasury of Yiddish Poetry*, edited by Irving Howe and Eliezar Greenberg, © 1969 Howe and Greenberg. Published by Holt, Rinehart & Winston Inc.

The poem by Abraham Reisen (Chapter 15) is taken from *The Golden Peacock*, edited by J. Leftwich. Published by Robert Anscombe & Co. Ltd.

The poem by Zbigniew Herbert (Chapter 2) is taken from *Modern European Verse*, edited by Dannie Abse and published by Vista Books.

Chapter One

Strange meeting

The world asks an old question:
Tra-la tra-di-ri-di-rom?
So the answer is: tra-di-ri-di-ri-lom,
Oy-ai, tra-di-ri-di-rom!
And if one wants to, one may also
   say: tra-i-dim?
So again we remain with the old
   question:
Tra-la-tra-di-ri-di-lom.

Yiddish riddle song

You can come to God in many ways. A student I knew read the *Summa* of Thomas Aquinas, said "that's it", threw up his career, changed his religion and became a priest. Julian of Norwich, in the Middle Ages, had a bad dose of 'flu, ran a temperature and saw visions. She lived on them for the rest of her life, and got herself walled up beside a Norwich church. She was noted for her common sense. Max Jacob, a surrealist poet, had a religious experience outside Sacré Coeur of all places, retired to an island and died in a concentration camp. A friend of mine switched from Trotsky to the Talmud and lives happily in an Orthodox Jewish Seminary. These came to religion by the front door, chauffeured by faith, certainty and visions.

With me it has not been like that. I've lurched and stumbled into belief, and bumped into God not only in places set aside for that purpose, but also in places to which nice religious persons don't go. In this book I have tried to give an honest account of what happened, and have taken off about six veils. The seventh remains firmly on, and so does the fig leaf over my private parts (though it has to slip occasionally).

I have written it for people like me, who do not come through the religious front door but who see if the backdoor to heaven is unlocked, or who try a window like the thief in the night mentioned in the Bible. It can be used by real unbelievers, who are becoming scarce now and are curious about what it is like being an animal inside the religious zoo, wired off from reality by faith. It can be used on the other hand by religious professionals, who earn their living out of the God business (like me) and who have some very uncomfortable and inconvenient doubts. It can also be used by masses of people, lurching, doubting, and bumping into the infinite, who would quite like a journey to heaven but who do not want to get taken for a ride. It is the story of the inconsistent progress of one puzzled pilgrim – two steps forward and one step back.

Some information about me, the pilgrim in question:

At school I was called an unbelieving Jew, which was in fact true. I am now a very cautious believer, because I do not want to be religious cannon-fodder for anybody. This tendency has become stronger as I have become more professionally religious as well. Now, like many Jews, I am not cautious because I do not have the capacity to believe, but because like many Jews I am inclined to believe too much and too often, which, I suppose, is why we Jews are still here.

I shut my eyes and remember the kitchen table of my childhood. My grandmother believed, and she enjoyed it. She believed in God and wore a wig to please him. (As she tucked the housekeeping money under it, it was also useful, as in fact were most of her beliefs.) She believed in amulets for sickness and the evil eye, and, when I was a child, they did me good.

12

She was also rash enough to believe in people, and so she had a life of belief, suffering and happiness. She was never burnt out by bitterness nor racked by envy, so her superstitions served her well. My grandfather on the other hand took a high view of God and a low view of his fellow Jews. He prayed regularly but refused to pay regularly, so he was unpopular with his synagogue. By contrast, he took things generously and gave them to beggars, including my mother's violin as she was working her way triumphantly through *Liebestraum*. It was odd that someone so cynical should have been a disciple of Prince Kropotkin, bravely asserting that the species helped each other to survive, which they might do in the Siberian forests he had left, but did not do so obviously in the East London dockland where he lived.

Then there were the assorted relations and friends, who gathered round my grandfather while he repaired shoes, and my grandmother when she made dumplings. I listened to them very carefully as a child, because, as they explained, they did not believe – they knew! Scientifically, like at school. They backed their knowledge with their lives, joining the noble army of secular saints and martyrs for materialism. Some of them were anarchist and returned to the East which they had left in childhood. They went to help the republic of goodness, which had got a bit confused, and we never heard of them again. I wonder what happened to their eager goodness, minced by the Stalinist machine. Well, they were told scientifically what would happen, by another crony who followed Trotsky. He was a little man who carried a great red banner. When the police came, everyone scuttled into houses and he was left out in the cold – the banner wouldn't go through the door – to take the consequences. When Trotsky was brained by an assassin, my childhood-friend gave up his beliefs and took to business instead. He is, I think, successful but nostalgic. Other relations and friends migrated to Spain during the civil war, did what they thought was their duty, and

13

when they did not come back, a great-aunt's hair turned white, and a woman in our street who had long memories of childhood pogroms went mad, gently but firmly. The thirties were so disastrous that it was a reasonable response. I thought of my cousins recently as I sat in a cafe in Alicante, contentedly smoking a cigar and sipping cheap brandy, remembering that this was the Spain which Franco had built, and which they had given their lives to destroy. I wondered if their sacrifice was necessary. There was no solution to that one and I ordered another brandy, for such questions lead nowhere. On the church across the road there was a plaque to all the nuns shot by the Reds. I have come to like nuns and it reinforced the point.

I looked on a turbulent world, fascinated and frightened by the amount of goodness and absurdity in it. My father was a decent man, a strong and silent type, a gentleman with a rare and terrible temper for injustice. We were walking down Mile End, and my father saw a coloured man being thrown out of a pub. My father sailed in wearing his best suit, his arms flailing. There was uproar and the proprietor got knocked out. As he came to, he opened one eye and looked tenderly at my father. *"Heshl!,"* he said in Yiddish, "do you know why I was throwing the darkie out of the pub?" "No," said my father defensively. "Well, he was making anti-semitic remarks." It was unanswerable and he closed his eye. "I told you so," said my mother, mortified beyond endurance. It was like an Amen. I thought about it for a long time.

My father taught me swimming and he taught me sin. I still enjoy the first, but am truly grateful for the second lesson. To Christian readers the sin is not very terrible, to orthodox Jewish ones it still is. He was an inarticulate man, and through layers of embarrassment he asked me to come with him and not tell the family. We trudged in silence through dark and devious alleys and came to a shop where they sold jellied eels, strictly forbidden in Jewish Law. There were only men there,

14

and it was my father's only escape from the meshes of matriarchy and tradition which governed our lives. He had suffered the dole and the loss of his dignity. He also knew that as I became more educated I would grow away from him. Before I had completely gone beyond recall, he took me to his private place, the only one he had. He was respected there, he recovered his manhood, and he talked. The truth which is not always welcome in liturgy could shine out among jellied eels. Should I give him away? I had a battle between priggishness and common sense. Thank God common sense won, and it is the only way I like to remember him now.

From this warm chaos I learnt a number of things. I learnt that reality was real and very solid. You could dream what you liked, but it would not change. I knew that no prayers would get people off the trains to concentration camps, and wishing would never make it so, despite religion or popular songs; it was the same syrup whether it came in full canonicals or from a juke box. When Mosley marched through the East End I prayed very hard. He didn't get through, but I gave the credit to my father who landed in hospital, my grandfather who landed in the arms of the police, and my grandmother's old cronies who carried buckets of water to throw from first-floor windows in Aldgate. My frightened piety had more to do with pixies and garden gnomes, and even as a child I never took it seriously. This suspicion of piety has remained with me.

All the revolutionaries I knew were very certain and very contradictory, like different parties in Judaism or in the Anglican Church. But they all respected this solid quality of matter, and therefore, somewhat regretfully, about the age of seven, I opted for secularism and sociology. In my heart I knew it had less colour but more truth.

I have never departed from this view of the universe. In theory it can be as hard as nails or as soft as a dream. The former is more natural to me because I was conditioned by a Jewish environment, not a Hindu one. It also inclined me

15

later to Freud, not Jung, and to an understanding of sex, not archetypes.

I only really came back to religion many years later, when I understood that reality does not have to evaporate in order to become religious. Also I did not need to spiritualize things away, I had only to sanctify and hallow what already existed. Neither the universe nor myself needed castration.

Another thing I learnt from those days was the beauty of belief and of commitment. Whatever the quality of the theologies and ideologies I heard around the kitchen table, they all had one thing in common: they took the members of my family, bootmakers and tailors, and on the dole, and gave each one greatness and integrity. The ideologies might not have been true in themselves, but they made their believers true, at least to themselves. It is unfortunate, but even very wrong and destructive ideologies and religions can elevate people. Some former Nazis, I know, are quite repentant but still feel that something left them which for a few years gave them a kind of terrible grandeur. I do not like this thought, but it is so. I have heard the battles of orthodox and progressive Jews, of orthodox and progressive communists, of disputes in the World Council of Churches, and realize how appalling and how ennobling is their passion, and how insoluble the issues.

I go to lunch with a businessman. The salmon is delicious, and he is a pleasant, cultivated man, but both of us are pragmatists. Neither of us would give our lives for the stock market or each other. Also, you do not invoke the Almighty in a city restaurant, so the salmon lacks a certain something. It is garnished but unblessed. It is expensive, it is out of season, but it is ordinary. There is a picture in the Rijksmuseum in Amsterdam in which a woman illumined by prayer and gratitude is bending over a slice of salmon on her kitchen table. She is transfigured; so is her fish.

I realized also, though I resented it and struggled against it,

16

that I could never become an orthodox Jew, or an orthodox Marxist, or an orthodox anything. What system could include Trotsky and Kropotkin, the Law and jellied eels, Marx and the middle class, and throw in "the God of my Fathers" for good measure? Such a system would have to be a fraud or infinite – a pious fraud would never do.

There is another memory from childhood which is the most difficult to tell, because I cannot even tell it to myself without feeling puzzled and foolish. Many years later I started to paint. Whatever picture I intended petered out, and I stopped being master of my own paint-brushes. They began to lead me instead. On the canvas an East End street appeared. It was about four o'clock in the afternoon. The fading light was late autumn or early spring. The street was a quiet one with some disused stables. A child was there – that was me – and facing him at the other end of the street was another figure. It was not an ordinary person and it was not a pixie, gnome, fairy, or Santa Claus either. It was real and profound; peace and love flowed from it, and knowledge too. I had wondered about death, though it was distant. The figure absorbed it. On the canvas the figure tries to shine, but my technique is not good enough.

I am sure there was some meeting but I do not know what. A Christian I know who saw the painting told me it was Jesus, and a Jungian I know told me it was an archetype. As a Freudian Jew I am less specific. But when I began to pray, many years later, I felt I was resuming a meeting or conversation that had been broken off many years ago. I knew who was at the other end of the line because we had met before.

I used to make light of it but now I take it according to its own feeling, which is not light.

Sitting in my office now, I administer one small office in one small section of the Jewish world. Occasionally I stand back, and ask what it is all built on, the synagogues, the appeals, the committees, the real estate and my salary. It all rests precariously, but very surely, on what Moses thought he saw in a burning bush, or in a dream of Jacob's, difficult as it is to disentangle him from Jewish pre-history. Gibbon said that the Papacy was built on a pun. In religion one has to get used to such slender but adequate supports.

Chapter Two

Angels on horseback

What is thy servant but a dog!

Ancient Semitic inscription

Come in peace you messengers of peace
Messengers from on high,
From the King above the King of kings
The Holy One – blessed be He!

Jewish Sabbath hymn to the angels

The Seventh Angel is completely different
even his name is different
Szemkel ..
Szemkel
Is black and nervous
and has been fined many times for
illegal import of sinners ..

Zbigniew Herbert

Abraham entertaineth three angels
And he lifted up his eyes and looked and, lo, three men stood
by him and when he saw them he ran to meet them ... and
bowed himself toward the ground.

Genesis

Jewish children receive much love, but little protection from
the world. All its tragedies and difficulties were discussed in

my presence, and while I sat on loving laps I heard no lullabies but the daily struggles of life instead – politics and unemployment, and the problems of marriage. As a result, I had no time for Snow White or the Sugar-Plum Fairy, and the only story that ever made sense in London's East End was Hans Andersen's Little Match Girl. In their place I had something odder but real – the angels – and they have been companions for the rest of my life. I was pleased to help get them back into the liturgy of my synagogue.

As a Jew, I was not used to pictures of religious facts or beings, and my angels had no haloes or wings, and wore no nighties. They were the *mal'achim*, the *angeloi*, the messengers one encountered in one's life who were sent by God. They helped me to cross frontiers, to face what was new, to see the world afresh. Three men met Abraham once: they were significant, they were his angels. Modern Jews get very puritanical about mediators. They want to face infinity directly. I cannot, it is too vast, too dark. I still need angels in my daily life; in prayer I can still talk to them though it took me years to get over the embarrassment, and I am grateful for their presence, whoever and whatever they are.

The "angel" who brought me release in my childhood was a Yiddish-speaking horse. She was an ordinary horse and I think her name was Bessie. I do not remember her master's name, but he was a cheerful old Cockney who liked Jews at a time when we needed it and never got very much of it. He taught Bessie Yiddish and, provided it was spoken in a Cockney accent, she understood it. When he shouted *"Shteh"* she stopped, and when he shouted *"Geh"* she began to clip-clop through the East End streets. As she came through Whitechapel I joined a gathering of Jewish schoolchildren and we ran before her, heralding her arrival in excited Hebrew and Yiddish and assorted Slavonic tongues. Many years later, when I heard the Gospels read in church, I always mentally put Bessie in the entry into Jerusalem. I also imagined her in a sequel – walking slowly and wearily to the knacker's yard, unheralded and unloved.

I suppose her master was really the "angel", but who can know who is the significant instrument or messenger from the beyond?

This Cockney genuinely tried to understand the subtleties of Jewish life. He knew my grandmother never suffered pain but only "egony", he bravely bit into unfamiliar foods, and lit the fire for us on winter Sabbaths when it was forbidden for us to do so. He understood the anxiety and justified paranoia which ran through Jewish life.

My great-grandparents had been killed in pogroms. Their children had fled and saved their lives, but they were not saved from their own fears. In the 'thirties the streets of London were sharply divided. There were communist streets, and there were fascist streets. There were alleys where no Jewish child could go and others where a good gentile ensured a safe passage (another angel?).

After the Sabbath was out, we used to prepare for our weekly excursion. We could either go to a salt-beef bar in our area; it was Jewish and it was safe, and my aunt might meet suitable young men there, chaperoned by her family. Away in the West End of London were the Corner Houses, glittering with lights and marble, and with glamorous little orchestras. As I have said, it was not an easy time, for the waves of fear and terror were returning as the first refugees arrived from Germany with tales of shame and humiliation. Should we stay among ourselves or venture beyond Aldgate Pump into "real" England? We needed reassurance. Sometimes we heard the Yiddish horse in the distance and it gave us, I think, that little extra courage we needed to meet gentiles.

In my life I have met other angels, and an unlikely lot they are. An angel can be the first person you fall in love with, who lets you down gently and lightly and helps you go forward into the risks of light and love. You can hear one in a bus queue whose name you will never know, but who says something which answers some inner questions, some need which is barely understood. It can be that intimate and strange figure, one's guardian angel. The analyst who came to my aid at a party was a messenger to me of deep significance. So was a charwoman, so was a Carmelite nun I only saw behind a grille. So was an East End horse. Understanding one's own, defending one's own and loving one's own are natural. Through a few creatures, human or animal, we are redeemed from our limitations and learn to meet what is strange and unfamiliar, and this is not quite natural – it is a little more, therefore it is supernatural. It is the only other religious lesson that has stayed with me from that period.

I stress that all this is real for me still, though such beliefs are not in fashion either in the religious or in the secular world in which I move. If it helps anyone, I willingly accept the mythical quality of my angels, though they are mostly very solid. The acceptance of them has meant that the incidents of my life are not accidents for me; they are clues to a meaning I sometimes grasp but cannot keep. These clues do not just form inside me, they are waiting there for me in external reality – if I can reach them.

Events in themselves are not this meaning; they are just the clues to it. Like words, they have to be read. When I later became a Rabbi and people came to see me, I believed their words at first. I did not read through them because I did not know how to. Soon I realized that what they said pointed to something deeper. This is so in conversation, in reading the Scriptures, and through events. I realized this as a child when I met my angel, and I am coming to realize it again. I did not realize it so well in my teens and twenties.

Moments of truth can appear in many ways when the meaning is sensed. You are standing at a cocktail party. In one hand you are holding a drink and in the other a piece of asparagus, your mouth is occupied in polite conversation. And

22

yet you have moved outside yourself and watch yourself dispassionately from somewhere near the ceiling above.

Sometimes too, after prayer perhaps, you see a familiar object as if for the first time, and it seems perfect and right.

A bridge game clarified the situation for me. It was late at night at another party. I sat near the players and looked at their cards. There was a tension between two of them – a husband and wife – which puzzled me. He was trying to win, and the more he succeeded the more angry she became, though it was hidden anger. I pieced the reasons together from their conversation. The man was playing against his employer. The more he won at the game of cards, the more he angered his employer and lost in the game of life and livelihood. He had focused his emotions and feelings, his success and failure, on two-dimensional cardboard, and it was real enough in a two-dimensional way. His wife had focused her emotions and feelings, her success and failure, on three-dimensional objects of metal and stone – freezers, cars and garages. But success in two-dimensional reality meant failure in three-dimensional reality, as she realized. He realized it too after a resounding slam. He looked at her in triumph. She looked at him with irritation, and he sagged as he readjusted to the realities of three-dimensional life and the triumph blew out of him.

I watched, and saw how the reality of cards was enclosed within the more inclusive reality of life and how the logic of one ran counter to the other. But the reality of life itself is enclosed within the greater reality of eternal life, and we can only dimly sense its meaning, and its demands. Devices (or realities) like angels are whispers we recognize, pointing to this profounder reality which encloses our own life as our life encloses a game of bridge.

Chapter Three

Confirmed

I don't care if it rains or freezes
  I am safe in the arms of Jesus.
I am Jesus' little lamb!
  . . .
  Hymn (censored playground version)

There ain't no flies on the lamb of God.

  Evelyn Waugh

Round the corners of the world I turn
more and more about the world I learn
All the new things that I see
just keep travelling along with me!

  Sydney Carter

I cannot write about the last war very well, because it was too
big and I was too small, and for me it had no continuity, just
one puzzle succeeding another. Like other evacuees from
Stepney, I wandered aimlessly round the country, dropping
into apprehensive households and equally suddenly dropping
out again. There were about sixteen in all, and they were all
respectable but some were not well-off. There were some
upper-middle-class houses too, but most of them did not
want our widow's mite and knew how to avoid us.

I ate my first non-kosher sausage. It was fascinating,
fearsome and tasty. I decided to give up belief and have
bacon instead, but belief would not give me up. It came with

the bacon and had an equally exotic flavour. I was in the messianic world of evangelical Christianity. One couple I met believed that the devil travelled on radio waves, and all the members of another family had been "born again". One lady had been washed in redeeming blood, which made me feel ill, and another buttressed a "four-square gospel chapel", which was too square for me. I marched with Rechabites against the demon drink, singing lustily:

> My drink is water bright
> from the crystal stream.

I sang this ditty to my grandfather; he clouted me, gave me some vodka and arranged Hebrew lessons for me with an old Polish cantor who was sodden in tradition and whisky. I never really thought a sausage was sin, and masturbation was just another unexplained muddle. (I had been reading Dennis Wheatley and got it mixed up with Black Magic.) But it was the march which disturbed me, because in Stepney my family and friends had marched not only on their feet but in their hearts, and I had marched not giving a damn about the demon drink, for it or against it. I had broken faith and this was sin. It seems small in retrospect, after so many years of jazzed-up protests, illicit indignation and synthetic provocation. But I had tasted the real revolution of working-class people, and in this area at any rate I still had standards.

The new religion did not take. Unlike the tattered remains of my childhood Judaism it had no style. The cabbage was soggy and drab, and it did not even deserve the chilly blessing it got. Also I liked results and could not see them. A mean man who would not let me read his newspaper told me God had taken him apart and put him together again. As he still did not let me read his newspaper, I could not see the difference. But some things remained. I realized that religion need not necessarily be communal, but could be personal, and I learnt a hymn of John Bunyan's, which I still sing. It is straight and clean with no bleeding lambs or pathos. My grandfather and the revolutionaries, all the good people I knew, could have sung it as well.

Being Jewish and lapsed, I was fair game for conversion. It was not cricket, and my new friends instinctively knew it, but they would have had to have been angels to resist the temptation. It was the first time anybody had tried to save my soul, and apart from the cinema with Carmen Miranda it was my only treat. At first I was surprised, then I realized I enjoyed it and led them on. It was useful practice, for spiritual coquetry is not so different from the ordinary kind, and I was fat at puberty and needed some polish.

Another conundrum was my confirmation, my Bar Mitzvah. I was yanked back to Judaism and to London in order to become a man. I learnt to chant some paragraphs from Leviticus, and saw where the gore of my "foster-mothers" had come from. It was my debut in the synagogue and was reckoned a success. My aunts got some fish for the party (there was a war on), and I got some savings certificates and a fountain pen. God alone knows what He got out of it! There was an odd sequel: A few days afterwards I was sent to the synagogue to thank the Rabbi. He was busy and I wandered into the empty synagogue to wait for him. Synagogues, like mosques, are often stark and the ark was closed. There was nothing there, it was empty and silent. But it was a friendly nothing, and a kind of loving was coiled in the silence. I surrendered to it and once again there was a meeting.

Though I later composed liturgy, it has always for me been a second best. Services can be friendly and kind like the crowds at Margate or Blackpool, but the theatre is always in them. It is silence which is the centre.

I was now in some strange archaic legal sense a man. The gory bits of Leviticus had done it, though how I could not guess. I experimented for myself in the back rows of cinemas, and learnt in the murk the different designs of boys and girls and where our entrances and exits were located. From the back row of the cinema I agreed with Noel Coward – it could have been organized better. How badly it was organized I scarcely guessed.

At a youth club I fell in love. We exchanged phone numbers, we would get in touch. I waited beside the telephone for many days, all feeling drained out of me. He never phoned. It was adolescent, but as awful as anything I have ever known. I may not have "become a man", but at least I became an adult.

Chapter Four

Religion in the ruins

For our Jewish life devastated
I pray to You, oh God!
I weep for Mother Vilna,
For Kolomec and for Brod.

For every Jewish brothel
that stood in a non-Jewish town,
For all that once was ours,
and now has been burnt down.

They are all so lovely, things Jewish!
our impoverished life rebuild!
And speak the word that is wanting
that our anguish may be stilled!

Zisha Landau

When I got back to London after the war there was a hole where our house had stood and there was a hole where my life had been. There was also a hole inside me too. I cannot describe the hole in my feelings as I hardly understood it myself.

Houses are replaceable, homes never can be. I wandered around the bombed streets, the boarded-up synagogues, and knew that the Yiddish world of my childhood was dying – perhaps it was dead. The great edifice of law and tradition and language had been crumbling when I marched off in the evacuation lines, but without the war it would, I think, have lasted out my time. This crumbling has of course not stopped. A few "Torah true"' Jews still effectively link such things as kosher clothing and the other details of Jewish life with the Will of God. Without this link there is no unifying and validating principle for all this – much of it bizarre. Either He cares or He doesn't, and if He is not that interested, well? There has since been an attempt to shore up the edifice without charismatics or theology by giving communal and human foundations to a teaching from heaven. Among Jews terms like commandment and covenant have been edged out by such words as Jewish identity, culture and ethnicity. As a bridging exercise the new terms have their uses until something better comes along. But they are all backward-looking, and it would be sad if the family of Israel became just another folklore troupe.

Our kitchen had faithfully registered the dying tremors of this old world. Even before the war we had begun to eat in genteel but gentile establishments in the West End, but only after the Sabbath was out and never meat. It is true that the jellied eels entered my father's stomach but they never entered his house, and he cleaned his teeth afterwards. In our kitchen meat dishes and milk dishes were strictly separate, as our Jewish tradition demands. After the war started another box lay just outside the door in the yard, and we now had three divisions: meat, milk and forbidden. Then came a bomb and it blew the milk into the meat and everything was forbidden. We were expecting an invasion, and never got round to sorting them out, so the bomb deconsecrated our kitchen and set our lives in a trajectory which led us outside tradition and outside God, though we still did not touch rabbit.

The signs of decay were everywhere. A Yiddish poet, who had written only ten years before for millions, now wrote for a loyal elderly remnant. His language had become "classic" in his own lifetime. He slept, I was told, on park benches. His readers had literally gone up in smoke in the camps. An old man used to sing the songs of Zion in the local markets, among the street traders – songs of Vilna and poverty, with digs at drunken cantors and over-righteous Rabbis, songs about the questions of working people to the Holy One, blessed be He. One day he was no longer there, and his songs had vanished too. The traders could hum the tunes but they could not remember the salty words any more. No one had thought of recording them, for no one had thought a culture could die so quickly. And it was the same with Yiddish theatres, and Yiddish newspapers, and mystical Rabbis, true and false and in between, and professional mourners, and marriage brokers, and taxi drivers learning Talmud at five o'clock in the morning. I heard the last sigh of the godly and exciting wind which had blown like a gale through the Jewish villages of Eastern Europe and had now dwindled to a gentle ghost – though a holy ghost – in London far away.

I walked through the ruins of Jewish Stepney, and I walked through the ruins of a world. It was a time for feelings on the grand scale. But an inconvenient question danced in my mind and punctured them as they welled up. Would I rebuild this world if I could? If someone offered me a return ticket would I accept it? I had seen my world from the outside and knew its limitations, and it was no use pretending not to know what you already knew. Lots of religious people try it, but the only result is banality. Many Jews feel this loss. Years later in Nice or New York or Hampstead I used to hear people say "do you remember?" and nostalgia threatened to drown us all. But Jews are realists – they have to be – and few of us would choose to go back to that pious poverty.

All believing groups suffer from nostalgia, and a past piety floats before them in a sentimental glow. It is either eighteenth-century Vilna, or the primitive Church, or the Tridentine Mass, or the caliphate, or the Odessa Steps sequence. Thank God time cannot reverse.

I certainly did not intend to fill the emptiness with religion. Between me and organized religion there was the Holocaust. The stories of suffering which filtered through to London, the tragedies of friends and relations, had burnt into me. It was not a question of whether I believed in organized religion. I did not even respect it. Like most young people's, my judgment was simple and ruthless. Some religious individuals had come out with honour, but their organizations, their Churches, chapels and liturgies had not. For a decade evil had reigned in Europe, and the organizations had compromised themselves out of credibility. They had been tested and found wanting. Both Protestants and Catholics had been invited to sup with the devil, and had accepted. I had not much confidence in my own brand either. If the Nazis had just shot gypsies and beheaded homosexuals, I think Rabbis would have attended that satanic dinner party too. Communists, socialists, atheists, and patriots like Churchill seemed more consistent.

The facts were beginning to be known in the late 'forties, and it was clear that everything in sight had been blessed by some godly organization or other. Concentration camp guards had sung Christmas carols, Popes had signed concordats with Hitler and Mussolini, and the Protestant State Church in Germany had expelled Jews who had believed in Christ. It was not that religious people were any worse than other people. The horrifying fact was that they were the same.

There was a whitewashing job going on of course, but it was pathetic – too little and too late. Even Stalin had got a religious blessing, and so had Franco, and Pétain, and every paranoid, evil or weak person in that testing time.

This suspicion of religious institutions has remained with me ever since. I have lost the anger now because I know when I search my heart that I would not have been very different, probably no different at all. And there is a Nazi inside me too: religion has taught me this. In other ways the hurt is deeper,

31

because when I did become part of a religious institution, the sin seemed even worse, it was not only wicked, it was also blasphemy against the Holy Spirit.

Only a thin line of true people still prevent a collapse of belief in me: Leo Baeck, the last Chief Rabbi of Germany; Anne Frank; that irritating Jewess Simone Weil; Maximilian Kolbe; Dietrich Bonhoeffer and Edith Stein; the Jewish doctors in the concentration camps; the verger of an Austrian church, who was executed because he saw that it was an unrighteous war and he did not wish to fight in it. (The religious authorities thought he was a fool.)

Many years later this antipathy returned in full force. I wandered into a church which stood near some railway lines leading to a former concentration camp. I sat thinking of the prayers that had been said in that church in the 'forties, the slight changes in liturgy that had been anxiously debated, the meetings of the women's guild. All this had taken place while the terrible cargo of human suffering was passing by on the railway tracks, and there was no connection. The religious engine did not connect up with reality – the clutch did not work.

The churches, the houses of worship, the synagogues of Europe, are still I suppose the places which can exorcize, which can transmute bitterness and hatred and turn suspicion into trust. But they are old, they are inefficient, and in the war many ceased to do their work.

Those years had needed prophecy and were fobbed off with piety. They were black and white years. Such colours were obvious, and religion had only to confirm them. Copies of *Der Stürmer* were after all available to anyone. Today the situation is different. The blacks and whites have merged into various shades of grey, and nothing is what it seems, for packaging is more ingenious. Who knows who stands for peace, liberation, equality, democracy and freedom? Who can tell the genuine from the false? In this situation simplistic prophecy is no help. The sound of words is so different from the taste they leave behind, but few can analyse the break. For me the real danger now is packaged thinking – this is the greatest danger to the soul, but a very subtle one for it can come in traditional and radical flavours.

At that time though, and against evil on that scale, rosaries, prayer straps and praying beads were toys, not weapons. It is of course easy to see the problem in others and not to see it in oneself. Among young Jews in the last few years I have noticed a revival in personal piety. Even among Jewish progressives, fringes dangle from shirt tails, a patch of coloured wool on the head is "in" and almost "chic". They are fine provided such externals lead to inner piety, and inner piety leads to prayer, and prayer leads to courage to face such impious problems as the wounds which divide Muslims and Jews and the needs of Palestinian refugees. I get frightened because reality gets lost on the way.

A contemplative, who is a friend, wrote to me that I believed in the God I experienced, but that he believed in what he had not experienced. For me this is dangerous. With that you can become cannon-fodder for anyone or anything – including the Devil – his Devil, I do not believe in one. But if he exists, he must sound pretty convincing, and up to all the tricks which go down well with religious people.

Chapter Five

Blue and white, and red

The colours of our flag are blue and white.

The Flag of Israel

The people's flag is deepest red,
it shrouded oft our martyred dead.

The Red Flag

Red, white and blue,
what do we think of you?

Popular song

Since I could not organize myself, I decided to organize the world. Since I could not embrace a friend, I would have to make do with Fraternity. Since there was no place for God, mankind would have to take His place instead.

If Christians do not believe in Christ, there is not much left. But if you are a Jew, without the God of your fathers, there is still quite a lot of débris around. There are memories of insults and spicy foods, and odds and ends of culture, and the antisemitism of the world outside, crude or polite, religious or political, left or right.

Many young Jews like me had to face this equation:

Judaism minus God = ?

What did a secular religion mean? What could you worship, and how did you worship it? I thought of the answers in colours, as I argued it out in my mind.

You did not feel chosen, but you did feel special (our recent history was very special and very nasty), and so you headed for the blue and white banners of Zionism. But you were also a descendant of the prophets – the old Hebrew ones like Amos and Hosea, and the secular Jewish ones like Emma Goldman and Rosa Luxemburg, and even the baptized Jewish ones like Marx. So there was another colour as well, the red flag "of our martyred dead" – the red of revolution, of hope and of my old acquaintance the Messiah, now dressed up in dungarees. Sentimental Christians take the Messiah, put him in a nightie, slap on some costume jewellery and turn him into an Icon. Secular Jews take off his halo, put him in overalls, give him a banner and set him marching.

I warmed to the blue and white, and to the red. I joined youth movements and wore different coloured shirts (chosen for ideology, not for taste). As I was a fast worker, I sometimes wore two ideologies at the same time, and must have looked, theoretically at least, like my ancestor Joseph with his coat of many colours. I enjoyed youth movements. I had a tepid respect for liberty and equality, but fraternity really turned me on.

I stopped wearing ties. I shared my pocket money, and did not dance the tango because the man "led" the woman and this was not right, and in any case I could not learn the steps. I also wagged my head and criticized my parents for their bourgeois habits, which was very satisfactory (they had at last made it out of Stepney, into a semi in Golders Green). I thought of becoming a pioneer, with a craggy look like Abraham Lincoln, brooding cheerfully over the promised land. I wrote an appalling patriotic play, which even gave my comrades indigestion and got laughed off the boards. For many of my friends this ideal was a true one, and their lives to this day witness to it. For me it was not.

The proof of the pudding is in the eating. So I learnt when I wrote a cookery book many years later, and it is the same with ideology as with food. I liked my promised lands from afar. Close up, they did not live up to their promises.

I went to Israel twice, but only felt at home with some odd and earnest surrealists I picked up, and a displaced Arab who tried to pick me up. The architecture was Bauhaus or pre-historic, and I could not relate to either. I cried with relief when I got back to England and saw Victorian houses in the rain. No one in Israel seemed to approve of Yiddish either. I was a Jew, I knew it. I had no "identity crisis", but the Jewish world in which I had my roots had been murdered or had died. I accepted this reluctantly, for it made me a displaced person, but there was a reward for honesty – freedom!

The red part, too, at that time did not bear close inspection. The Communist Manifesto of 1848 is a truly noble document, and I am pleased that I managed to smuggle a phrase of it into a prayer book. Classes do exist, and so does their struggle, and so does the connection between overpro-duction, imperialism and disaster. But Stalin had just butchered the Jewish intelligentsia and shot his doctors, and though some of my friends loyally soldiered on, I thought it more scientific and more Marxist to see the obvious.

I am not a Zionist now, but it did give me back another Jewish culture, when my own brand had gone. I ceased to be one, I suppose, because it had no direct relationship to my adolescent needs or questions. I was not born in Eastern Europe with its endemic anti-semitism and its dangerous mixture of religion, nationalism and culture. Unlike many of my colleagues and friends I had never experienced a con-centration camp or labour camp or political anti-semitism. I had only experienced the social kind with its hurtful remarks. I do not know how I would feel if the events of the 'thirties and 'forties were repeated. Another reason was that I knew I could locate most unpurified passions in myself and this separated me from most ideologies. I had a short period of sado-masochistic phantasies in early adolescence. If they had grown, and taken political form, I could have been in jackboots too. I was also exhilarated by words and rhetoric, and found I could enjoy them passively, and actively. I was therefore inoculated against all gut reactions. Later on, the connection between theology and politics worried me, but not at that time.

Zionism helped me to stop playing games with myself about anti-semitism – "It could never happen here!" It could happen anywhere. I am not a Marxist either, certainly not the middle-class kind fascinated by dogma and destruction like a rabbit by a snake. But a lot of it has passed out of the world of my "isms" into the world of my common sense. I am pleased I was a Marxist, for religious people ignore it at their peril. My present community may have its heart in the promised land, and its soul in the world to come, but its cheque stubs and mortgages belong firmly to the bourgeoisie.

There was another experience which helped me on my way: a puzzling one. Whenever I approached a promised land it began to look more and more like the world I had left behind. It is an odd sensation to stride into the future and step back into your past. Yet this is what seems to happen. Some friends in Eastern Europe wanted to show off their new society. They refused to let me eat in a "workers' caff ", which really interested me, and took me instead to a posh restaurant. Their pride was justified: the food was good, the waiters wore tails and the wines were expensive. It was like the "Trocadero" of my childhood and all the Lyons Corner Houses I have ever known. The marble, the coat tails and the fiddlers had gone East.

The established kibbutzim I visited were cheerful, friendly, hard-working places. They were thriving and would soon blossom into something like Golders Green – which I was trying to leave. Neither society seemed to tolerate either God or porn.

In Tel Aviv a nice frank lesbian told me with resignation of her experience among the revolutionaries. (She had gone to a very left-wing kibbutz indeed.)

"Like girls? Sure, we all like girls."

"Love girls? Sure, we all love girls."

"You can't want to. . . . Where do you put what? (thought, not said) . . . nice to have you . . . don't come back."

She would have had a thin time of it in a workers' paradise as well. It is fair to say of course that all these societies have become more tolerant in recent years, but then so has the bourgeoisie as well.

There was another doubt on a deeper level. Our adolescent aggressions and lives were used by ideology, but ideology did not transform them. The world might change, but I had the uncomfortable feeling that we would not. What would it be like to be an imperfect person in a perfected world? Could we enjoy it? I once spoke of it to my youth group leader. My feelings were irrelevant, he said, only the social purpose was important. I assented to please him, but it did not satisfy me. I worried over it. If we built the good society, would the society make us good too – a bonus like trading stamps?

Another thing that disturbed me was the manipulation of feelings. The source of my feelings were personal and sexual; their expression was political. I remember passionate speeches at public meetings. The expression of them would have been more honest with whispers in bed.

It was obvious that things were not right. The treason trials were beginning in the East, and the Palestinians were in their camps. A young girl who was a communist told me later that in the Stalin period the dialectic had got distorted by personal factors. In other words the revolution had been hijacked by fear, greed and ambition. Since social ideologies dislike "inner truth" which they find "subjective", I think it must always be so. I remember a revolutionary pageant. I rushed out on to the stage, and declared that I was the "Spirit of Fighting Indonesia!" The audience approved, but I felt a fraud. My fervour came from my clumsiness on the dance floor, and my aggression from rejection. In my heart of hearts I knew I did not love the world; I did not even like it. In a muzzy way, I realized I had better begin to like myself – and take some dancing lessons.

In memory, I stood again, a child on that silent street at that meeting long ago – if it was a meeting, that is. When I thought of it, the acting stopped, and Abraham Lincoln and the Spirit of Fighting Indonesia crumpled up like puppets without a master. I knew I would have to learn to love myself before I could love the world, or even another human being – if I could find one, that is.

Chapter Six

A Trollope

Before a child is born, a light is held
behind its head with which it can see
from one end of the world to the other,
and they teach it the whole of the Torah.
But at the moment of birth an angel
touches it on the lips, and it forgets all.
So all of life is spent remembering
what we once knew.

A story from the Talmud

And is it true? And is it true,
   This most tremendous tale of all,
   Seen in a stained glass window hue,
   A baby in an ox's stall?

John Betjeman

I never became a pioneer, but I managed to avoid becoming a solicitor (or an accountant, or a dentist, or a company director, or any other job suitable for a bright Jewish boy). I compromised with my parents, and according to the compromise's terms found myself in Oxford, wearing a "bum freezer", and studying the Venerable Bede. My parents never suspected how such a venerable and dead gentleman could cause so much upheaval in a Jewish youngster. But he did – and I was deeply moved by his sober account of the wayward Celtic Christianity which had once swept over northern England. It was the first time I had ever thought that the history of non-Jews could be holy.

There were rumours in Hampstead that I had gone soft and betrayed the cause – or the causes, since I was always quite catholic. I had also been seen at Anglican services. A nice gentleman travelled up to see me. He was Marxist and Zionist, and I felt uneasy. He was conscience and nemesis. I decided to brazen it out. We went to dinner, and I hurriedly discussed apostolic succession and the claims of the Anglican Church. He must have thought I was dotty, and I certainly felt a trollop in a Trollope world. (Marxism had me rather puritan, like my wartime landladies in their four-square gospel halls.) If he had seen enough Humphrey Bogart films he would have said, "How come a dame like you in a dump like dis?"

Though he never expressed it in those terms, I felt it keenly, and wondered furtively what a Yiddishe boy like me had to do with such gentile baubles. The truth was that they fascinated me. Christianity is a mystery religion in a way that Judaism is not, and I was fascinated by the incense, the sacred choreography, the weird Book of Revelation, immaculate conceptions and virgin births. I had never met anything like it, and I was flabbergasted.

It had the attraction of forbidden things: of blasphemy, High Church and low porn at the same time. Devotees of festivals of light should remember that for many non-believers, they are like purveyors of opium to the masses, spiritual drug pushers in fact.

When he left, puzzled and disappointed, I tried to give the answer to myself which I had not given him. Oxford – the university, that is – disappointed me. History was kings and barons, or, in other words, cops and robbers, or cowboys and indians. Why bother to waste time on the inner deals of a medieval Mafia! Al Capone seemed more relevant. I liked my tutors, and they put up with me politely and kindly but they disclaimed wisdom so hard that I unwillingly had to believe them. They were very understated and more English than they knew.

Culture, I thought, should be more adventurous than this. There were lectures on Anglo-Saxon charters, and tutorials by an expert in Scottish seal cases. There was no sex because Oxford was at that time a one-sex society, and that sex was forbidden. To relieve the tedium there was the New Left, which was just beginning. It might have seemed New to a public school boy but not to an East End kid with my childhood. Also, it seemed to have gone a bit sour. There was the aggression without the passion, and it was still pretty puritan. Later on the desire for "happenings" began to show itself more nakedly, and the movement became more thrilling and more destructive. It also seemed to me not exactly phony, but pastiche – the middle class playing at revolution – rather like artificially-weathered jeans (working-class around the crotch) or Chinese boiler suits, tight-fitting and tailored. The only things that puzzled me in the entire town were the spires and churches. What on earth were they there for, and who on earth went into them?

One Thursday, I passed a Quaker meeting house, when a meeting was about to take place. It was not for undergraduates who came on Sunday but for Quaker farmers in the country round about. I walked in, sat down, and was sucked into the silence. It is the only mystery the Quakers possess, but it is a very powerful one. Some people got up from time to time and said the normal things, reminding the Almighty of the more distressing current events as if He did not know them. I did not bother about them. I wanted to go deeper into that silence, because I knew that something was in it. It was the same silence I had felt in synagogue after my Bar Mitzvah. I had picked up an old thread, and I was jolly well going to follow it and unravel it. I attended that meeting every week for about two months, and the silence became deeper and more profound. It began to have a face, a personality and a voice. At one meeting I spoke as well, because it spoke in me. That was my first and last testimony. It must have sounded genuine because the chairman of the meeting came up to me, deeply moved by my words. I was more suspicious and decided Jews should not become Quakers, they were too garrulous.

I was puzzled, and decided to explore this odd phenomenon. I went to the Jewish society, but as they were mainly interested in kosher meals and Israel, I only went there when I was hungry. As my interests became known, I was also invited to cocoa parties with the godly, who were fascinating but sexless. I enjoyed the religious one-upmanship though, the ecclesiastical gossip, and the high camp of it all.

To return to the real thing, I began to wander into church crypts at odd hours of the day on the off-chance that something might happen. I suppose it was meditation, but it seemed like conversation. Then the effects of it began. Something very odd occurred, and it set me back on my heels. Despite the stillness of it all, I rediscovered love. I had lost the power to love in my childhood, and now it had come back. I did not give a hoot who Jesus was, but the parables of the kingdom hit me with their off beat truth like hammer blows. I was in a bus and the people ceased to be human cattle on their way to work, but souls on their way to eternity. I suddenly found the delight you can get from giving things up. Jesus and the saints invaded my prayer life, and I saw the world transformed. Every lover sees it that way, but I did not realize I was in love. I still thought that to love you needed sex and a human being. They help, but are not necessary and can get in the way.

I gave someone my new tie, and tried to give up everything to everybody. My intentions were misunderstood and the consequences were embarrassing. The Dean was puzzled, and warned me against overdoing it, though neither of us were quite sure what "it" was. Another tutor bawled to me over the quad, enquiring, What religion was I up to now? Again I was embarrassed because I did not know.

I did know that some other changes had taken place. I began to feel young again and frolicsome. Religion was rejuvenating. Somewhere in the cosmos there was a point which was not malevolent or neutral, and I began to take a brighter view of my prospects. I felt quite sure it would not let me down, whatever it was, and in a suspicious way I began to trust. Up to now I had been a grim and grubby undergraduate. I was still grubby because I had not integrated my body into all this, but the grimness began to dissolve. The cosmos seemed less heavy with tragic lumps. It was now lighter, like a soufflé, and laughter gurgled through it. I wondered if I was a mystic or just a manic depressive on a high. Humour was the last thing I ever expected from a religious experience, though I should have known better, because my childhood Judaism was laced with it, like alcohol.

My ecclesiastical progress got higher and higher, as I proceeded from mystery to mystery. I read bits of the Gospels, and progressed in a dazed fashion from miracle to miracle, from the incarnation, to the transfiguration, and then on to the resurrection and the ascension. I could not make it out. I took a Jewish girl friend to a church, and we went round the stations of the cross. She was fascinated as well, and said it reminded her of Madame Tussaud's. It did me too.

That is how I ended up in an Anglican monastery at Easter time. I really felt at home. I loved the morning prayers as the cold light came through the windows, the friendly and blessed quiet, the sudden glimpse of a light that shone beneath the surface of things like the light that shines through the fragile skin of Rembrandt's old people. But I had gone ahead of myself, and did not know how the rest of me could catch up. There was so much that could not be said – at least I thought it could not be said. If you masturbated, for example, did it matter, and whom could you tell? It seemed to be taken for granted that I was going to be baptized. A converted Jew would be the cherry on the cake for Easter devotions. I felt like a lamb waiting for the slaughter, or a widow in India about to jump on her husband's funeral pyre. A monk took me aside and told me that I would like to know the difference between English Catholics and Roman Catholics. I had never thought about it – they were all gentiles, weren't they!

Suddenly several people intervened. The elderly Bishop of Borneo said he would not baptize me or confirm me (he was a wise man).

A relative said she was going to commit suicide if I brought such shame on the family.

My parents telephoned and said I was doing it to spite them.

I think I would have still gone ahead if I had believed. But I was beginning to get indigestion because I have no aptitude for belief. I came to the verge of baptism because I was suffering, and Christianity gives meaning to suffering. It also opened up spiritual vistas, and it helped me to realize that my own centre was not located in this world. Christian belief could also express a spiritual love affair "medieval style" in modern theological terms, and for this I am still grateful.

I withdrew from the verge because I felt I ought to solve my problems before I tried to transcend them. A lot of them could be dealt with in terms of this world. It was not right to invoke another until this had been done. Also although Christianity opened up vistas of love as I have said, it muddled up sex more than ever.

Also, the anti-Jewish elements in it were unacknowledged, and therefore still dangerous.

It was all too much and too puzzling, and I decided to have a breakdown and see what happened.

Chapter Seven

The truth that makes you free

Truth is our king, the rest is nothing.
Forms of prayer for Jewish worship

And the truth shall make you free.

New Testament

. . . he merely told
the unhappy Present to recite the Past
   like a poetry lesson till sooner
or later it faltered at the line where

long ago the accusations had begun,
and suddenly knew by whom it had been judged,
   how rich life had been and how silly,
and was life-forgiven and more humble,

able to approach the Future as a friend
without a wardrobe of excuses . . .
W.H. Auden ("In Memory of Sigmund Freud")

Coming from a line of Jews who had to be tough to survive, I
found it was not as easy to have a breakdown as I thought. I
could not help just getting through exams or going to a party
just when I had decided to go into an institution. I was very
unhappy despite the light which had flared up again at the
Quaker meeting. And I did not trust that light either. I

suspected it was all frustrated sex, and one night of love, human love, would dispel all that divine dottiness.

Many years later, when I spoke about those years to a slightly younger friend in Berlin, he looked at me with tenderness. "God," he said, "how all of you must have suffered in the pre-Pill generation!" I was moved to tears. I had suffered; adolescence was hell if you had any sexual problem or hang-up, and I felt very sorry for myself. Religious people have a habit of whining about the selfishness and corruption of the present, and compare it to some golden past which is known to them but not to me. I wish I had been born ten years later, and missed Mosley marching through the East End, the Nazis, and the awful isolation and ignorance of puberty. My father was a regular subscriber to the *News of the World*, and I read with avid interest of *femmes fatales* and wicked old men who were waiting to pounce on a boy like me. The one pounce that did take place excited my pity but not my pleasure. The newspaper assured me that those fiends were everywhere, but not where I happened to be – to my secret regret at the time.

There was an awful lot of self-pity in me. It oozed out at a party in Soho. I was alone in one of the rooms, and sang the blues to myself – an old number of Bessie Smith's. It was one of those parties where people stick candles in Chianti bottles to give the gloom a gay, southern look, and I had not noticed a man in the murk. He was such a nondescript man too, who looked as if he would fade into the biscuit-painted walls. His voice was nasal with a slight Cockney twang, and he told me brusquely to come around next morning at eleven o'clock. My analysis had begun.

I have never understood the geography of the analytic world. It is partly my fault. I have never learnt the difference between a counsellor, a psycho-therapist, a psychologist, a psychoanalyst or a psychiatrist. They seem to have a strong sense of hierarchy like the angels around the celestial throne,

47

and take umbrage if you mix them up. It is partly their fault too. Freudians, Jungians, Adlerians and Kleinians seem to be always splitting like amoebae and reforming – like splinter parties in Israel, or exclusive groups of the elect. They form committees and issue manifestoes like all the groups of devotees I have ever met: surrealist, Marxist or religious. But alas "the wind passeth over them, and knoweth them no more".

The next morning, to my surprise, he did not start off with a cosy chat, nor did we discuss my mind or soul. He asked me to lie down on a divan, and told me to take deep breaths and learn to expel the air in my body. He then gently massaged some muscles in my neck and chest. I burst into tears, and leapt into a trauma of early childhood. Since the Quaker meeting and the re-appearance of the flickering light, I knew something would happen, but I never expected enlightenment to come through my body. Sometimes a session could last nearly twelve hours, and I leapt through trauma like a performing seal, feeling as naked as a skinned rabbit, though more hopeful. (One hour sessions, so common in conventional analysis, might be economic, but not therapeutic.)

He was a follower of Wilhelm Reich – Freud's most brilliant and heretical pupil. I tried to read the Master himself, but my mind could not master the system. It needed a knowledge of anatomy which I did not possess. My analyst told me that reading was unnecessary; feeling and tasting the flavour of my feelings was the important thing. A certain amount I did get to know in a puzzled way. My mind could lie, but the tensions in my body did not lie. My soul could play tricks; the instinctive responses of my body did not. In the geography of my flesh was the plan of my past and the hope for my future.

Against this approach I had no defence. I had no shell, and for moments and hours which seemed outside time I not only remembered but also re-lived the experiences which had taken away my innocence and freedom and turned me into an old and wizened theoretician.

I spoke to him about my religion. I spoke aggressively, because I did not really believe in it. In my heart of hearts I never thought it could survive such probing. He told me that if it was neurotic, it would not survive (I was frightened to face the loneliness and emptiness of the cosmos once again). If it was not neurotic, it would. There was no more comfort than that.

I was one of the few people I knew who stuck it to the end. In the prayer book there is a phrase that "Truth is our King". Truth was holy, and cloud-cuckoo-land was silly, and blasphemy too. Swearing is not saying four-letter words, but denying what is. There is also a sentence in Marcus Aurelius which stuck in my mind, because it was bed-rock. "If there is a God, follow him, if there is no God, be thou godlike!" It is the only beginning.

Jeremiah had cried "my bowels, my bowels" and I cried "my body, my body!" Neither Zionists nor Marxists nor Quakers nor Catholics of any variety had shown me this path. This was new. I did not like it, but liking is a luxury, respect is not. Sooner or later in religion a stripping is required and a darkness must be faced. This stripping takes many forms. It is the "sacrifice of truth" mentioned in the Jewish liturgy. If we are religious, such a sacrifice can never finish. It can only deepen. Prayer means that God is speaking. His voice demands, and it demands a change within us. If it does not, then the exercise is pointless and we are left as imprisoned as before within our limitations. In youth or adolescence the sacrifice often means giving without strings to a cause, to a person or to an ideal. Later on it develops into that special type of giving, which is giving up. Giving up the illusions about the same cause, person or ideal we had given so much to before. As we approach death, of course, we have to give up something more than illusions. The stripping, the sacrifice, changes its form, but it is always there. It seems unpleasant, but without it religion becomes both very easy and very cheap.

There are many places where the sacrifice of truth can be made; mine was on a divan in a council flat. But the New Testament says "the truth shall make you free" – if you want to be free. Fortunately I had too much pride and need to turn back. God helps the poor in spirit, and that is what you have to be for analysis to work.

The analysis ended abruptly just before my final examinations. I telephoned to make an appointment as usual, and he answered that there would be none. Perhaps we could meet each other socially after my finals were over. A panic swept over me. I would not be able to get by, I shouted over the telephone. He answered that I knew as much about myself now as I could know, and that analysis was no substitute for living. I was quite a toughie, he said. "No I am not," I answered angrily. He wished me good luck and told me I would get by, and I did.

After the analysis ended, he went to India to an ashram. A deep metaphysical problem, he said, underlay all the problems of the psyche and the ego. This surprised me, for he was a Freudian and read the *Daily Worker*. He never claimed to be a Hindu, only a Vedantist, and I did not know what that meant. I looked it up and found he was a monist, not a monotheist. A monotheist believes in a God, though only one; a monist believes in the oneness of everybody and everything. A friend of mine once jokingly said that he was only a pimple on the backside of eternity (the actual words were more vivid and cruder). I decided I could not follow my analyst there, as I did not like talking to myself, especially in prayer. Like my ancestors Abraham, Isaac and Jacob, I did not mind a fight or a defeat, but it must be with a being – not with an idea and not with the All.

There is a lot of kitsch in religion – especially in the traditional ones. In this episode there was none, for truth by itself seems cold.

Chapter Eight

My excluded middle

Whose love is given over-well
Shall look on Helen's face in hell.
Whilst they whose love is thin and wise
May view John Knox in paradise.

Dorothy Parker

After all this I had to think of me. Who was I and what was I?
What was I made of, what did I consist of? I wasn't very sure
who I was, or indeed if I was at all. I had had to wear so many
masks that I no longer knew what lay beneath the masks, if
anything. The only real things were the sense of inner pain
and loss, and the strange clues I had stumbled across which
puzzled me but pointed somewhere. The ideologies and religious systems I knew were not helpful here, they were too
materialist and Western. They got impatient if the worshipper
turned away from questioning the existence and identity of
God – "theology" – and began to ask the same questions
about himself. I found a Hindu centre more to the point. My
most important religious task at this time was finding out who
I was or at least a reasonably accurate hypothesis on which I
could work and act. This identity problem was not artificial or
trendy; the bewilderment was real – it hurt!

I had read about "the destruction of the I" in spirituality
books, and I was interested because all forms of destruction
are fascinating – whether it is a car crash, or a house on fire,
or blowing up a society, or the ego. There is an agreeable

excitement about such things. The question "what am I?" actually occurs in the Jewish morning prayers, but it is treated as a rhetorical question among a lot of others, and no minister I knew ever paused at that point.

In the book of Leviticus there is the sentence "You shall love your neighbour as you love yourself". There is a sharp Rabbinical comment that this implies you must first love yourself or be in charity with yourself before you can start trying out your love on others. I had learnt this myself the hard way, before I ever read the commentary. But this led to another question: what was this self I was supposed to love?

Until my analysis I had never dared to tackle this problem because I had never liked myself. Whether his theories were right or wrong, my analyst did like me and this gave me enough confidence to start. When I say he liked me, I mean the "me" that actually existed, not the masks I wore – the bright boy, the good son, the committed Jew, or an addition to the baptismal font. I have always been more interested in the analyst's commitment than in his theories or symbols. A bit of real fondness for the "real" person goes a long way.

In my mind I decided to give a party and invite the various bits of me to it. If I was not going to have another breakdown, they would have to meet some time and learn to put up with each other. Although God made me a unity, for the sake of convenience I thought of myself as a kind of trinity. There was my mind, my soul and my body, and a meeting was arranged.

It was an uncomfortable gathering, and it was a triumph of my analysis that they could come together at all. All three, after all, had tried to murder one another. I had used my mind to kill my feelings. In my imagination it had grudgingly allowed a bit of culture, but it had tried to dissect love, not to understand it, and no living heart can survive such an operation. It had tried to confine the things that brought me life, and stunted both my natural flesh and my supernatural

God. For many years it had excluded all other parts of me, and those years had known success, but it was bitter and tasteless.

My soul had played a subtler game. On the outside it looked gentle enough – most religion does – but it had subtle and lethal weapons of its own. It tried to poison my mind by feeding it things it could never stomach: specious logic, foolish phantasies and pointless miracles and happenings. After I had tried to follow my soul, I had ended up by being able to believe anything – the more absurd it was the better. A friend of mine had sailed into that sea of paradoxes and had committed suicide. I had no intention of doing likewise.

Both my mind and soul, however, could combine if necessary against the third guest, and their union was theology. Like many marriages of convenience the attachment came from shared hatred or fear, not from shared love.

This third guest, my body, was the me that had suffered most, whose needs and cries had been heeded least. My mind had despised it and my soul had mortified it. Under the strain it had almost broken and no longer wished to live – one could scarcely blame it. A kind of respectable suicide is not uncommon in certain forms of religion. A priest I know runs a counselling centre for other priests and monks and nuns. There are enough cases of ministers who have drunk themselves into oblivion and nuns who have starved their bodies into anorexia.

Bodies are not genteel objects, with their desires, their smells and their hair, but they too are God's creation and, in tradition at least, were given their share of glory. "I believe in the resurrection of the body," says the Christian creed. "Blessed are You Lord, who puts life in dead bodies," says the Jewish prayer book. In the nineteenth century the resurrection of the body was replaced in many "progressive" liturgies by the immortality of the soul. Souls are so much nicer than bodies and are tidier theologically too.

At the dinner party in my mind, my body is the least welcome guest, and it is so in many religions. The body has to be left outside the door before the mind and soul can enter. In a sermon one can scarcely refer to its useful and necessary functions.

Anything or anybody who is rejected or threatened behaves like an animal at bay, and the body is no exception. Its natural expression of love cannot always be sublimated, and its rejected energy goes sour and flows into illicit ambition and power which poison religious structures. I remember sitting in a church listening to a long and involved sermon which attempted to spiritualize away the brotherhood of Jesus and James. It seemed a dirty trick on James. There is a certain amount of material about Mary as a mother, but what on earth was she like as a wife? Most religious institutions would, I think, prefer their clientele to be disembodied and to be beyond all four-letter words. Unfortunately all the words are in the *Oxford English Dictionary* – that is the way God arranged it.

My body is not just a lump of meat. It thinks, and has its own insight. Many times it came to my aid when my mind and my soul could not help me. I was in a train at night, surrounded by Arabs making their long way home to Morocco. Our politics and our religions were separated by two decades of misunderstanding and political animosity. It was hunger which brought us together, not theology or ideology; common hunger and the desire to have a little taste of what the other person was eating.

In Germany after the war I met fellow Jews and little groups of liberals. In Hamburg once, as I lay in bed, I listened to a story I had never heard before, and had to comfort a former enemy. Only our bodies could create the intimacy and the trust for such an exchange. It was more effective than sharing a pulpit.

I was told that, in the discos of Jerusalem, Arab boys dance with Jewish girls. They are curious about each other, and opposites attract, which is as it should be. I think I was meant to deplore such goings-on like the speaker. It seemed to me that when religion becomes fanatical, and minds are warped by wars and nationalism, only bodies keep their sanity. They are basic and not articulate, but at least their thoughts come straight, if only they have been given a little love.

Chapter Nine

The Call

And I heard the voice of the Lord
saying Whom shall I send, and who
will go for us? Then said I, Here am
I; send me.

Isaiah

Becoming a Rabbi? Become a dentist instead!
That's no job for a Yiddishe boy.

Popular Jewish opinion

My call did not come from an angel, it came from an advert. I
was approaching the end of my university career and was
becoming a bit uneasy about the future of a graduate with
second-class honours and first-class aspirations. I no longer
wanted to drain a swamp in Israel or water a desert. Nor did I
wish to be completely respectable like a solicitor or an
accountant. During my analysis I had started painting. Some
of my pictures were exhibited, and kind friends bought them.
A review said, "Mr Blue contributes a loud and strident note
to an otherwise quiet and restrained exhibition", and I
seriously wondered whether to become an artist.

Looking back on it my cheek was colossal. As I read the
advertisement I asked myself which was greater – to create
works of art or to be a work of art. In an unsteady way I lighted
on the latter (God help me!) and answered the advertisement.

I have forgotten the words, but it was a polite request for

suitable young Jews with university qualifications to come forward and present themselves for a rewarding career in the Jewish ministry. It came from a part of the Jewish world I had never met before: anglicized, ethical and middle-class. I had been more Anglican than anglicized, I was not middle-class but *déclassé*, and some mystical moments would have to take the place of outstanding ethical achievement. I was not going to mention the analysis.

By correspondence we decided we were suited for each other, but as in all dating systems we had to meet.

I visited the synagogues where I would have a rewarding ministry. One reminded me uneasily of a bank. At another some impersonal prayers were gently recited at me, and from the roof a choir sighed "Amen". At another the accent was so thick that I could not understand a word and felt more hopeful. I assumed it was Hebrew, but the wardens insisted proudly that their service was in the vernacular. I sent a polite letter calling it off, and quickly received an even politer one agreeing. A good family friend who was a frustrated Rabbi urged me to try again, and I wandered on, a dispirited pilgrim through the temples of Jewish suburbia.

I was not smitten by any of them, but I did take to one Rabbi very much, and disliked his services least. He was human, inconsistent when it did not matter, and warm and supportive when it did. He had a temper, but did not bear a grudge. His sermons had lovely beginnings, but no endings. He worked intuitively in religious matters, and I amused him. He was a good man who did not think religion was just morality heightened by emotion – if anything it was the other way round.

Over the years my attitude to progressive Jewish services of whatever variety has changed. This is not because I later edited some of the new liturgy and composed some of its prayers, but because something in me changed too. I realized that Jews had not lived on the moon and had been more influenced by their surroundings than they cared to acknowledge. The "Authentic" Judaism of my childhood years was orthodox, and was suspiciously like the Orthodox Church in its attitudes, with the same mixture of long liturgy, warm piety and a heady combination of saintliness, dottiness and superstition. The resemblance was hardly surprising because we all crept out of the same marshes in White Russia. The Judaism I now encountered was of German provenance, *punktlich* and theological. Services started on time and almost ended on time, with only half an hour's lee-way. (Thank God they were still Jews!) The dominating operatic cantor had been replaced by a sentimental warble from some unseen grating, and the Slavonic groans had been civilized by Mendelssohn. They did not seem to care what I ate, but they did care about what I had read. Gastronomy was out, theology was in. Fortunately the theology was mostly in German, and, as everyone said it was so great as to be untranslatable, I did not have to read much of it. Like most lapsed members of an ancient tradition, I was on the horns of a dilemma. I could not go back to the past, and did not like the future. To see if I was doing the right thing, I paid a flying visit to an old-time *Yeshivah* (a traditional centre of Jewish learning). They were kind, pious and consistent. I loved them very dearly, and now knew definitely that I should have to opt for the chilly embrace of Jewish nonconformity. At the beginning it worried me a great deal. Later on I realized that most religious problems are matters of taste and style. Do you like religion penny plain or tuppence coloured? Do you wish to sit or to stand? Both have their advantages and disadvantages. Does the Holy, blessed be He, prefer the former or the latter? Perhaps He likes variety – after all, He created it.

I went before a selection board. I was prepared to defend my vocation, though there were some shaky bits. I think they felt as shaky as I did about such high and mystical matters. My accent was right, mainly Oxford though under stress I turned final English "g"s into Yiddish "k"s! I seemed to be reasonably clean-living (I had had neither the opportunity nor the know-how to be anything else). Moreover I was prepared to stay in England. They had had two previous students, and both had been sent to study in the promised land across the Atlantic, not the Mediterranean. I was agreeably surprised by my examiners too. They did not seem like saints, but they were gentlemen, and courteous, and it seemed a fair exchange. I had known Judaism *à la russe*; now I was prepared to taste it *à l'anglaise*. I suppose that they also did not have much choice. The old seminaries had died in Berlin and Breslau, though one had kept going till 1941. The changing sociology of Jewish life was sweeping large chunks of East European Judaism into a Western stream, and parts of orthodoxy were collapsing into progress and bewilderment. I was just a symptom of a great change which was taking place in Jewish life. But it is easier to devote one's life to fanaticism than to liberalism, so liberally-inclined Rabbinical students were in short supply. The flat earth society is after all more committed to its flatness than I am to its roundness.

I was accepted. It was not exactly a love affair, but there was real satisfaction on my part. Once again I had a Jewish home – or perhaps not exactly a home as yet but a *pied-à-terre*. It was more than I had expected. The Rabbis said very rightly that love does not come at the beginning of a relationship, but at its end. It is the reward of a shared experience, the usual irritations and commitment. That is how it happened with me.

My vocation caused a stir in my family. My parents were puzzled. They had tried so hard to get out of the ghetto, and here was I going back into it. What were my motives? they asked suspiciously.

A neighbour congratulated my father on the honour he had received by my "call". My father was perplexed and my mother disconcerted. In their confusion they got in touch with my grandfather, who got in touch with his bosom drinking companion, an old ironic cantor, with more than eighty years of experience. My grandfather rang back. The cantor had said this: "Mr Goldstein, I am an old-time Jew who sings his guts out for God the whole week, and what do I get for it? Your grandson is on to a good thing. All he has to do," he added wistfully, "is to say some bits and pieces in English once a week, and he'll make a fortune." My grandfather told my parents firmly not to stand in my way. It was heretical, but it made sense, and it is a hard life being a Jew. For the record, the cantor was too optimistic. Only my blood pressure has risen, not my fortune.

My "call" lacked refinement, but it has stood the test of time. Synagogues and Jews have sometimes irritated me beyond endurance, and I have been unable to sleep at night through worry or annoyance. I am sure I gave them some sleepless hours too. But despite the rows and the arguments, a hidden elastic draws us back to each other, and this is what a "call" is about. Like most marriages it has had its ups and downs, but it is a marriage, not an affair.

The only thing it lacked was romance. I had read the autobiography of Thomas Merton, the Trappist monk. He describes a moment when he seemed to hear the tolling bells of Gethsemani Monastery calling him to a life of penance and silence. It is a moving story, and I was frightened when I read it, lest those awful bells should toll for me as well. As, with all my vagaries, I have usually gone where prayer seems to lead me (two steps forward, one step backwards), I had good reason to be apprehensive. Thank God they did not toll for me.

I say all this because I do not ask prayer to lead me very far. Practically speaking, it works best if I am thinking of the next step ahead. When the situation becomes less precise, the prayer becomes less pure. The discipline of prayer arises naturally out of its use, not out of a textbook. It certainly needs a discipline because otherwise there is little to stop multiplying blessings for all and sundry, one's friends and enemies (forced), one's colleagues and cats (fervent). Inflated prayers are no different from inflated money, a lot of them gets you (or anybody else) very little.

In any case the next step ahead involves everything that matters. You can build your religious life out of such little steps, if you choose. The textbook for this approach is *Self-Abandonment to Divine Providence* by a French eighteenth-century Jesuit. Similar ground is also covered by the Chassidic Rabbis in eighteenth- and nineteenth-century Po-land.

My "call", as I have said, lacked romance, but as my grandfather used to say, "if a horse drops from heaven, don't examine its teeth". He was a bright boy, he was.

Chapter Ten

Wrong reasons for the right thing

Rabbi Zadok says: Do not use the Torah as a crown for your own importance or a spade to dig with.

Sayings of the Fathers (Talmud)

And Joseph said unto them (his brethren), Fear not, for am I in the place of God?
But as for you, ye thought evil against me: but God meant it unto good . . .

Genesis

When I decided to become a Rabbi, I felt guilty because I had done the right thing for the wrong reasons. I no longer think right or wrong reasons important. Just as you cannot simulate a marriage, you cannot simulate a religious commitment either. You can call it a leap of faith or a pig in a poke, but you do not know what you are in for, until you are in it. It is not why you go in that is important, but what happens to you when you are in.

Some people I know commit themselves in one leap of faith to a religious organization and their problem is living with the consequence of that leap in the years to come. I am not a spiritual high-flyer. My family had stalls in a market, and England at its best has always been a nation of shopkeepers. I retain a market trader's distrust, even when I deal in religious bargains. I am prepared to commit my ways to God if I have to, but I am not prepared to commit them to my fellow men, whatever robes they wear or whatever organizations they represent. This applies also to their Scriptures, their behaviour systems and their creeds. In spite of the fact that I have more and more regard for believers and their niceness, I prefer to learn from my own mistakes than from their successes – even if I have to pay the bill.

All the reasons I gave to the committee which accepted me were true. I did want to translate the warmth and kindness of my traditional Jewish childhood into modern life. I did know that cleverness was not enough and that underneath it was a wisdom which could master me but of which I could not be the master. I knew that Judaism was my home. I also was quite clear that where prayer led I had to follow.

I was also aware that there were a lot of other reasons too, and since they were shrewd men they must have been aware of them also. Later on, the tables turned, and it was my turn to sit on seminary admission boards and on religious courts hearing applications for conversion. The following is an uncomfortable list of the "wrong" reasons for coming to God or to the institutions which try to represent Him. Some of them were my own (some are still) and some are ones that even startled me. All of them combine with one another or with "right" reasons, whatever they might be.

Getting a job. As I have said before, a religious vocation is a strong motive for displaced intellectuals. It is even stronger if you have an arts degree and yearnings after infinity.

Marriage is a common one, and a great deal of my present work is concerned with it. I give an example. She is Jewish, and you are not. Her parents are causing trouble and are hunting you with tribal tomahawks unless you get circumcized fast and convert. Where can you find an incompetent Rabbi and a competent anaesthetist? ("Will it hurt?")

You are going to church or synagogue because you are a dutiful son or daughter. Over the years I have realized that you can use your piety to sock your parents one in the eye – especially if you decide to become a monk or a nun, or to enter a *Yeshivah*, or to convert. How on earth can they protest about your "vocation" – the swine! They instinctively feel the aggression in your devotion, but in face of the divine they are out-manoeuvred. There are many cases with this element, and the strategy, even if unconscious, compels my admiration.

Frustration in love or sex is very common too, and takes many forms. You cannot get a boy-friend or girl-friend, so you settle for a divine one because there are no human ones around. Though God is above sex, His representations are not, so be careful about the brand of religion you choose. If you want a divine girl-friend you are out of luck if you are a Jew or Protestant, and in luck if you are a Catholic or Hindu.

Another variant on this theme arises if you have fallen for your Rabbi, Pastor or Priest, and have confused him with the Almighty. It is rather like transference in psychoanalysis. (As many modern ministers consciously try to be attractive and with it, they can be accomplices too.) The result is that you yearn to worship with him and prefer incense to musky aftershave (or, with the ecclesiastical emancipation of women, to perfume).

Another backdoor to religion is business or status. Joining the right Church can put you in with the right people. In this context, "right" is more political than theological. In communal religions this aspect becomes quite important. You can become a churchwarden or synagogue councillor, and get status that way, or you can give large sums to religious charities and buy it. This is a problem for all middle-class religious set-ups where there are hardly any working class people, or if they exist they are the recipients of religion, not the donors – a sort of Marxism in reverse. Surveying the market however in a business-like way, I think becoming a Freemason would be more efficient. This is no aspersion on them, it is a side effect of their success – their hospitals, charities and mutual help are quite outstanding.

Sadness and sorrow are good diving-boards into the divine. More of religion is based on them than on virtue and happiness. As there are more great tragedies than there are great comedies, it is the easier option. It is easier to be depressed or aggressive than patiently to work through a problem and solve it. Broadcast prayers have a dying fall, and their subject-matter in the morning does not help people facing a new day with as much cheerfulness as they can muster. (Lord, turn thy gaze on Bangladesh and its starving millions ... Lord, we lay Northern Ireland and its problems before thee ... Lord ...) Sermons too have a querulous note. Even if the words betray some optimism, this is pricked by the mournful voice. This voice is worth noting, with its complaints and reproaches, because it has become a permanent feature of Western religion. Why this is so, I do not know. It is equally difficult to see how the common sense of Judaism and the freedom of the gospel resulted in all the sexual hang-ups and injustices of the early Middle Ages – yet a change took place in the first centuries of the Christian Era and it is not easy to account for it. Nietzsche saw clearly the weakness that underlay much religion. Like most young people I read Nietzsche and then abandoned him because he was too querulous and too one-sided. Later I had to consider him again, because so much conventional religion was based on weakness, keeping the devotees in an unnaturally pro- longed childish dependence and preventing their maturity. I have always liked the words of Ezekiel: "Stand on your own feet, and speak!" I like Job's arguments more than his sub- mission. If I could I should prefer to approach divine things from strength and happiness. As it happens, I can't most of the time and this is my own personal sin, a real one.

When people go to their dentist, their theology undergoes a profound change. People also pray when they are too embarrassed about their pains and problems: if they suspect they have got V.D. for instance, or are speedily about to become a one-parent family. *"In hac valle lacrimarum"* hits the nail on the head, and the "vale of tears" is very recognizable.

To continue the gloomy tale, self-deception comes quite high on the list. Life seems dull, and religion of the charismatic variety certainly hots it up a bit. Some people go into the ministry because they like hearing the sound of their own voice and think a congregation might get the same glow. Religion is good for rhetoric, echo and reverberation. From pulpits your voice can come back to you at all angles and at all volumes. You can turn it up crescendo (God) or you can turn it down diminuendo (humility, for example), and there is always some background wow and flutter provided by the choir. You can also deceive yourself at a deeper level. It is quite easy to visit a convent in the country, especially in summer, and decide to become a contemplative. There is a lot of knee-work, it is true, but there is no telephone, and you wear out less shoe-leather than running after the morning bus. You quite soon realize that what you need is a holiday, not a vocation. Thomas Merton says a contemplative monastery today is run on the lines of a munition factory in wartime. In the ones I visit an extraordinary amount of manual labour goes on. You have to have a vocation to be a navvy or a builder's labourer as well.

Wives predominate over husbands among the clientele of prayer. I suppose instinctively they want to make the nest more secure and stop their husbands straying. (Men predominate in pubs.) In these uncertain times a Roman Catholic ceremony is still the best glue available, but even that is no longer cosmic Araldite.

A great deal of a minister's work involves counselling, and the range extends from the disorganized to the dotty. Most people are a bit neurotic, but they find it easier to present their neurosis in theological terms. Divinity makes you a little more interesting, and it certainly covers a lot of dottiness. It gets more dangerous when religion is a vehicle for megalomaniacs. "Thou art That" and all that, or being part of the Mystical Body, or embodying the Jewish Problem.

A dangerous reason for becoming godly is to deepen one's nationalism or tribalism. It is a primitive and powerful combination. All detachment and holiness is gone when God is made to shout "up the Irish" (or the English), or authenticate uncertain rights to promised lands.

I end this grim and dismal list, though the variations on it are infinite. I have never met anybody in my life who has entered religion pure and uncontaminated by any of the above. I have met some people who thought they were not. I was curious about them. A few were liars, some had no insight about themselves and lacked self-awareness, others had hypnotized themselves out of truth.

Religion, real religion, begins when it can risk the truth. Conversion takes place when you can admit to yourself all the wrong reasons that are at work. For many years I tried to pretend to myself, and my God became pretence too and the awareness of Him make-believe. One day at a service, I said to myself, "To hell with it!", recognized the impurity in myself, and knew that I was not God's boy-scout. At that moment, when I became myself and admitted what I was, I could pray. At the time I thought my reasons for going into religion were important. Now I believe that, when I was brave enough to admit they were wrong reasons, I was right in applying. It sounds cockeyed, but the truth digs deeper than our conventions.

Chapter Eleven

Teach yourself God

Of making many books there is no end
and much study is a weariness of the flesh.

Ecclesiastes

An ignorant man cannot be pious.

Sayings of the Fathers (Talmud)

Fortunately – religion depends as little
upon theology as love upon phrenology.

Israel Zangwill

By the early 'fifties, the Jewish communities in Europe had regained a superficial normality. This was a minor miracle which few people saw at the time because all eyes were fixed on the greater drama of Israel. All over the continent, the survivors had come out of the concentration camps or out of hiding. They had reformed themselves into communities and built synagogues in the ruins of the greater Jewish world which had passed away before their eyes. Eighty per cent had died, many had "changed their country more often than their shoes", and the waves of immigration and dispersion had scarcely settled. East European "Yidden" were drifting back to a German "homeland". (Yiddish was after all a German dialect.) North African Jews were pouring into France. Everybody seemed to be on the move.

My Rabbi decided to recreate the old Jewish seminary of

Berlin in London. He did it partly because he believed in the Diaspora and partly to forestall another Rabbinical student and myself from straying. We were the only.two he had, and he was frightened we would go west. He seemed to proceed by intuition rather than by rule. This irked me and I told him so. He retorted how else could he put the bits and pieces of such a world together, and I had to admit it was the only way possible.

The "normality" covered an inner chaos. Like Humpty Dumpty the Jewish world in Europe had been smashed, and there was no master-plan for reassembling it. It had to grow like Topsy or as in Isaiah's words: "a little bit here and a little bit there". With great difficulty he assembled the scholars who had survived the holocaust. Improvisers cannot be choosers, so what I lost in consistency I gained in variety. While he was doing this, he sent me to learn Hebrew and Aramaic grammar to keep me out of mischief.

I certainly learnt to understand every variety of accent Central Europe could produce. My Hebrew grew passable, but my understanding of broken German was superb and Buber is still for me "Zee aye unt se Zou". Umlauts littered my mind. On every level there was a dilemma, because the world before the holocaust did not fit the world which followed it. My teachers had been trained for a world of reasoned tradition, but they had experienced an apocalypse instead. They had believed firmly in the goodness of men, and they had met evil in its most concentrated form. A liberalism which could survive that earned my respect, and I started being converted to the brand of Judaism I had joined.

But the training was very unsettling. One teacher tried to teach me in modern Hebrew, and the result was chaos. Another assumed I knew everything an old-time Rabbinical student knew – but I did not, I could not, and I knew it. English life did not fit me for such things. I was trained in Jewish law and spent years poring over codes. When I came to a congregation, I was never asked a legal question. I was educated to listen to one type of problem and was required to answer another.

As a student, I was tried out on a congregation. I sat proudly at my desk and waited for the first client. He showed up at midnight, and I never knew his name. He was going to commit suicide, he said, and what was I going to do about it? Nothing in my experience had trained me for this, and I suggested weakly that we have a cup of tea. We discussed various forms of suicide until the early hours, and both of us became quite animated. He then rose, told me the conversation had done him a power of good, and left abruptly, leaving one deflated and perplexed "Rabbi". I had learnt a little about governing a world, but there was no world for me to govern or pontificate over.

Even on the communal level, the answers did not fit the questions. Beneath the "normality" there had been a collapse in belief. Certain basic and crude questions stuck out like monoliths or tombstones, and what could one say about them? Where was God during the holocaust? Why had the prayers of the victims not been answered? Was Israel a compensation for the tragedy? The holocaust is now drifting into history, and we have all learnt to live with such questions, not to answer them. At that time I was desperately worried, because I thought I had to provide an answer for everything.

For the first time I began to realize what the burden of tradition was and how heavy it felt. It was not just a question of my own religious "experience"; I had to prepare myself to lead a community. I had to grow up and was not yet ready for it, so I criticized others instead.

As a student I was allowed to attend the meetings of the other Rabbis. They were Rabbiner Doktors, and some of them were Rabbiner Doktor Doktor. There was even one, I was told, who was Rabbiner Doktor[3]. They sat stiffly and gravely in their chairs, their folios open in front of them, and I sat at the back, seen but not heard.

What does learning religion mean? In study you can master texts and learn about religion, but you cannot get degrees in the things which matter. There are no doctorates in goodness. I suppose the best way is to mix with religious people and hope to catch "it" off them like measles.

I am grateful to my teachers, for they let me into their lives. I am even more grateful to those who were not afraid to let me into their weaknesses. I asked a traditional teacher what was the answer to biblical criticism. He hesitated, but was godly enough to tell me there wasn't one. It did not affect him too much, he said, but it did affect me. Another, who was a deeply displaced refugee, allowed me into his inner chaos. The heights and depths in it were staggering, for he was one of the few scholars of genius I have known. I learnt from him that the Creator of all this could not be a divine headmaster of a minor public school and that I could not be his prefect. He came along with me to a modern synagogue and listened with incredulity to a sermon about the Continental Sunday (against that desirable institution, of course). I felt deeply ashamed and decided to give heretical sermons if I must, but not silly ones.

The rich chaos of my education started producing an answering chaos inside me. Many of my teachers had looked into the abyss, and I had looked into them, and the abyss began to look into me. Unlike them I was not anchored to texts. I tried to swallow them, first uncritically and then oiled by criticism, but I only got indigestion both times. There was a real difference between us, and I did not know if it was personal or if it was a symptom of a generation gap. For them the sacred texts were at the centre of their religion. They were like rings of a tree. The revelation of the Books of Moses was surrounded by the books of the Bible, and around them was the great fence of the Talmud. Their lives were another commentary on these books, and they stood on the ramparts defending the tradition from a secular army. God was inside, and unbelief was outside.

71

To be an insider, you had to be pious, and I was only "pi", which meant that I was outside the fence and, in my heart of hearts, beyond the pale. In my brief moments of honesty, I had to admit that for me the sacred text was my life and my experience and that the Sacred Texts could only be a commentary on it. They might have the ultimate truth, but it was not my truth. When I accepted this, it was a relief. I no longer had to believe tall stories, and defend the Truth from anybody. If it is the Truth, it can look after itself. I did not have to worry either as to how biased it all was. Christian scholars were quite gleeful about dissecting the Pentateuch into E, J and P, with such elegant cuts as P_1 and P_2. The same scholars became much more pious when they approached the New Testament. I liked looking at the process both ways, because with Jews, of course, it was the reverse. They were good critics of the New Testament and good believers in the Old. But one thing was clear to me as I came into touch with the congregations. The sacred texts were receding over the horizon fast and none of the scholars could do much about it.

The spiritual realities might be the same in Manchester as in Moab, but you needed a lot of time and learning (and sleight of hand) to make the connection. Occasionally a cry of pain from Jeremiah or a devastating criticism of Isaiah would pierce through the liturgy into modern people's hearts, but mostly it was all too far away in time and in place. It was magnificent, but it was not close enough to be real. The other holy books had suffered an even worse fate, for they had ceased to be read. The Zohar, the foundation of Jewish Kabbalah, was unknown, and the Talmud was no longer a popular debating ground, it was only for the experts. The great code of Jewish Law, called the Prepared Table because it was specially designed in the sixteenth century as recommended reading for idiots, house-wives, minors, diceplayers and the similarly handicapped, now required a Rabbinic education to understand it.

I genuinely tried to be false in those years. I tried to disapprove of people breaking rules. I wagged my head over the impieties of youth, and I deplored the Continental Sunday. I gave feeling sermons about the Jewish Home. (They owed more to *Little Women* than anything I had ever known.) I also repeated all the right things, like how hard it was to go to Germany, how good it was to go to Israel, and I kept silent about the right things too. I never mentioned the Palestinian refugees, though that was the time when something could have been done. I never told my congregations the truths I had discovered during my psychoanalysis. Nor did I mention my occasional visits to Hindu gurus and Christian friends because I needed their help for prayer.

By chance I heard of a modern Dutch-Jewish writer. I got hold of some of his poems and they intrigued me. His name was Jacob Israel de Haan. He had a traditional childhood and was the son of a cantor. He had had girl-friends, had broken out into bohemia and had written a homosexual novel. Everybody assured me it was great, but it was also unobtainable because de Haan had got reconverted to traditional Judaism and nearly every copy had disappeared. He had then gone to Palestine as the teacher of the ultra-traditionalists, had suffered political disillusion and was shot in Jerusalem – nobody knows by whom. Perhaps it was personal, perhaps it was political. It happened in 1924 and there may be some people still living who should know, but they will not tell. His poems were too *fin de siècle* for me – they were too full of roses and lilies, but the man fascinated me.

At about the same time two other things happened. My body said it had been suppressed long enough, and my mind and soul had been undermined by scholarship. At a Talmud lesson, I started translating from the tractate which deals with all the hypothetical and phantasy questions connected with Jewish divorce law: "if a man writes a bill of divorce on a leaf and hands it to his wife . . ." I made an impertinent comment. My teacher reproved me. I answered back. We had a row. I sent in my resignation, and booked a place on a boat for Amsterdam. I was jolly well going to read that novel.

Chapter Twelve

Yes to everything

Die liebe dauert oder dauert nicht
   in dem oder jenem Ort.
(Love endures, or doesn't endure in this
   or any other place.)

Bertolt Brecht

Truly You are the one who probes
   and bears witness. You record and seal
You remember all that is forgotten.
You open the book of memory, and it
   speaks for itself, for every man
   has signed it by his life.

Day of Atonement prayer

I decided that I was going to say no to God and yes to everything else. I needed at least a holiday from religion, and the holiday could last a life-time as far as I cared. Such a holiday is not as simple as it sounds, in fact no holiday ever is. We might have nothing to lose but our chains of habit and responsibility, but we have become attached to them. They are also barriers which fence us off from experiences which have no bounds or limits and which are frightening. When they are gone there is nothing to protect us against great longings and desires, and routine cannot shelter us from God and our own selves. For many people, including myself, happiness can be frightening, and the straightforward search for it often beset with anxiety. Perhaps we get too accustomed to living in twilight, or perhaps we fear that when we have got it we shall no longer want it.

It took more courage to take this holiday than to enter a seminary. I am not sure what I feared most – that nothing would happen or that something or someone would happen, and neither of us would be adequate.

The Jewish world is a small world, and the Rabbi in Amsterdam knew I was arriving. He asked me if I could help him. I needed to help myself, and I told him so. He was a wise man, who wished me good luck and made no comment as I was sucked into the world of bars and discos and the underworld of meetings and happenings.

This great northern town made me drunk. (It is a town, not a city.) The skies were vast and I felt dizzy watching the lowering clouds and shifting lights. Great winds blew in from the North Sea, and I felt as if they were blowing all the silliness out of my life, the stuffy sermons and the false attitudes. It was a town with a clear and honest light, and I needed that clarity and honesty to enter into me.

All this took place over twenty years ago, and the world is now a trickier place and sins have become more subtle. At the time I thought "hash" was something you got in sandwich bars: sinful, as it was not kosher, but not illegal. By modern standards my revolt was small beer – the Provos, the hippies, flower power, marijuana teas and the squatters were still to come. Nevertheless I went to hell in my own way, and very satisfactory it was. I realized that I was a night person and adjusted accordingly. I used to sit by the Carlton Terrace in the evening at 7 (p.m. not a.m.) to eat my breakfast, and watched the town changing before my eyes. I speculated on what would happen to me that night, as I watched the day people taken home on the trams and the night people tentatively coming out to look over the streets they would occupy until dawn. The scholastic philosophies I had read had tried to put away experience in great filing cabinets. The quality of it did not matter provided it was filed. Aquinas had done this for Christians and Maimonides for Jews. I remembered that Maimonides had never found much sense or use for music or poetry either. Such unsettling things are necessary companions for both love and laughter. I wondered what would happen that evening. What doors would open, whose life I would enter and who would enter mine, whether it would be for a night or for eternity?

Some of it was silly, and some of it quite sleazy, but I am a bit too, and so are most people I know. My attempts at love were incompetent (I had little knowledge and even less practice) and I did not know the difference between what I should feel and what I did feel. Far more devastation was caused by my incompetence than by my wickedness. The fundamental sin was not one I had bothered about much in my formal religious education – self-honesty. Sex was neutral, hypocrisy was not.

It took me some time to realize what real sin and real virtue were. I had been so preoccupied with formal ones or synthetic ones. As with all other things in my life, I needed experience and teachers. I needed experience because I am not able to learn easily from other people's experience. Even though my mind knows the answer, my body has to work out the question. I needed teachers because it was all so chaotic. I could not see the obvious (it is always the most difficult thing to see), and on my own I could not purify myself, to stop myself from playing games.

Whenever I have asked for help it has seemed to come, though sometimes I have not been able to spot it. (In my childhood a carthorse was an angel.) In this period I studied under a number of "rabbis" who had never been ordained. But since Rabbi only means teacher, they deserved the title. I do not remember the names of many of them and have lost contact with them, and they have passed out of the light of my interest. Occasionally a story found its way home to me. Some may now be respectable businessmen, and one a pillar of society. None of them, I think, ever took religion seriously; one, a gentle and defeated transvestite, lost hope and committed suicide. Sometimes I mentioned my background. They were more tolerant than I expected (just as later on I found religious people nicer than their religions). Everyone had his own phantasy, they said, his own deviation. In love, some liked women, some liked men, some liked both, some liked . . . well, religion for example! Occasionally late at night with a cigarette in the darkness, my head on a pillow, I tried to bring the genuine things outside the holy ghetto and translate them into everyday or everynight language. I could do it at such a time and such a place because I needed intimacy for such intimate things. This helped me in later years in my office or in pulpits.

I no longer used "label" words like "redemption" or "salvation", unless I could identify them in experience and communicate that experience. I also recognized the unity of things, the profane threads in the holy and the holy in the profane. I looked at labels less and contents more. So I found spirituality in unexpected places: in Colette, for example, in Freud and in Brecht. Because I had drunk with a mixed bag of humanity, I found little difficulty in vaulting over theological hurdles, and praying with them as well. In fact prayer and drink go rather well together. Some Rabbis used to have schnapps before a service, and it certainly helps to remove that deadening self-consciousness and artificial language which mummify prayer. The ghetto walls which once seemed like a fortress now seemed like companionable ruins. Because they didn't prevent anything, I grew rather fond of them.

I needed to learn very simple things. I needed to learn for example that the drama never changes, the action is always the same and it is only the scenery which moves. In a seminary or in a bar, in the Rabbinate or in bed, there is the same struggle between what is generous and what is mean, what is good and what is expedient, what is right, I suppose, and what is wrong. In later years I represented respectable organizations in London and other cities. The scenery had changed dramatically – it was all "religious" – but little else had. My "rabbis" and angels had redeemed me from formalism.

Although I had said "no" to God, He did not appear to have said "no" to me. Sitting in a bar late at night I was deeply aware of His presence. I heard within myself His commentary on everything around me, and I knew that here was a gateway into the kingdom, perhaps the most obvious gate I have met. Although I was off all services, I was not off prayer, and the darkness and the detachment made it a very good place. I had some deep but quiet dark nights there, of the soul too.

The world can be seen in many ways: as tragic, comic, farce or whatever genre you like. Two or three perspectives on it are better than one. They are confusing, but one only confirms you in your own rightness too easily. It is a minister of religion's professional hazard. There was one bar I used to like, and I used to have a drink there before going home. It was a pick-up bar – where ministers did not go (unless to pick up). Since for many it represented their last chance of companionship against the loneliness of the night, everything always went quicker there. There was not enough time to act, so everything was more obvious. It was easy to see who could give and who could take, and who could do it with grace and generosity and who with bluff and brutality.

Some pick-ups showed real consideration and I hoped they would be able to have breakfast together on the morning after the night before – without love probably but with affection. Some were so corroded by fear and disillusion that one hoped they would not degrade each other too much. Occasionally some transvestites wandered in, but they wore the only fancy dress there, and it was not fancy dress for them, not like the robes, pompoms, black gowns and gaiters in churches or synagogues. Watching them, a Rabbinical voyeur in the corner, good and bad were so obvious to me. Nobody was arguing about lapsed food laws or Jewish identity or the Church of South India for that matter. I remembered a sentence of Plotinus I had stumbled over in my student days: "I have seen the nature of the good, and know that it is beautiful, and the nature of the bad and know that it is ugly." From then on all the sermons I gave were about what I knew and not what I had been told. I had tasted the flavour of both and the difference was unmistakable.

I ought to have gone to libraries and researched Jacob Israel de Haan and committed a thesis. I should have tracked down his novel. I never did because I did not have time for his lilies and roses and love affairs which were thirty or forty years old. I was too pre-occupied with the "book of life" and signing it with my own name.

Chapter Thirteen

Returning

The tavern will not corrupt a good man, nor
   will the House of Study straighten out a bad one.

Yiddish proverb

Lord of the world
I want to sing you a "You Song"
Where can one find You
And where can one not find You?
Wherever I go You are there, and wherever
   I stand You are there
Only You, just You, always You, ever You!

Rabbi Levi Yizchok

He was a busy man and a scholar and the journey was not easy
for him. When was I coming back? he asked. My Rabbi, he
said, had not sent in my resignation. He could only have one
of me, but one of me he had better have. I think my Rabbi
was, and is,. genuinely fond of me, and at that time there were
only two or three Rabbinical students, so I was better than
nothing. If I was away and my fellow had 'flu, the Seminary
might as well pack up, the lecturers could hardly lecture to
each other. My scholarship had continued to be paid, he said,
and I was expected to take Day of Atonement services in a few
weeks' time. I should hardly lack material, he added drily.

I decided it was useless speaking of my life; I should have to
show him. He trotted obediently after me as we plunged

through a collection of bars and discos ending up in a snack bar in the early morning. He asked the waiters to remove the ham: there were some barriers, he said, that he did not wish to cross.

We scarcely spoke; I gazed tenderly at him, especially when the tears began to trickle down his cheek. I knew I had to shock him, but I did not want to hurt him. Tradition is a heavy burden, and his back had bent under its weight. The tears flowed faster and suddenly I got suspicious, because he began to shake as well. To my annoyance and horror he was quivering and collapsing into laughter. He had enjoyed himself, he said. Had not laughed so much for years, difficult in fact to keep a straight face (I thought he had looked grim). Nothing like it since the Weimar Republic. Now, he said, when was I going to be a good boy and come back. The services had been arranged and he agreed my organization could only have one of me (certainly while it was so small) but one of me they had better have.

Very well, I had tried to live without my body, but could I live without my soul? – and my mind, he said, was not being very well catered for, either! I was not part of a romantic tradition, he added; I should learn to have my cake and eat it. This was what civilization was about anyway, but compromise required a good heart and a good mind if it was to work.

Everything he said made sense and touched me on a sensitive spot. I had not found love. I had in fact met it, and it had been offered me, but I was in too much of a hurry to see it. The relationship had real companionship, but we could only communicate with our bodies and sooner or later our bodies would be tired or jaded. What could we tell each other then, and how could we tell it? I could live in my work but not on sex. Absorbing though it is, it can only be a part-time activity. Also, my digestion could not stand up to eating breakfast at supper time for ever.

I could not give him a direct answer, and asked him to let

me think it out for a few days. Could I endure going back to a comfortable prison again, living in a community in which I had not yet found a place for my body or a *pied-à-terre* for my soul? I sat in my late-night bar and fingered my beads. An Arab had given me some prayer beads and a Catholic boy a rosary. As I did not have the slightest idea how you used them, I used to keep one or other in my pocket and finger the clicking beads to remember significant people or events, to recall the times I had encountered "angels" or experienced something. Religious experiences are so ghostly that, unless you tie them down with beads, they can be dismissed too easily and evaporate into the spirit from which they came.

With my beads I tried to recall the events of my religious training. One bead brought back a memory which surprised and refreshed me, though at the time it shocked me. A scholar I knew, to illustrate the beauty of old Hebrew style, had asked me to translate a paragraph or two. Part of it went something like this: A woman had come to a Rabbi and asked him the following question: "I laid the table for my husband, but he insisted on turning it over. Is it permitted?" To this the Rabbi replied that it was unusual and that she should try to lead her husband back to more normal ways. But if she could not, the table would have to remain turned.

It was an odd passage, and another scholar reproved the one who showed it to me for leading me astray. With the beads I had remembered it, and it did not lead me astray, it led me back to Judaism. I had never heard the subject so delicately stated, without losing any precision, or without silly excuses. I realized that out of necessity I had not made a good compromise. I had tried to be too "good", and on the rebound too "bad". Neither was real. I could only make a good compromise by being what I was, and, in the business I was in, it had to be a holy compromise. Compromise was not even the right word. Perhaps marriage was better. I had to marry together all the truth I had found or tripped over, all the experience which had been injected or had percolated into me. The marriage would have to join the wings of angels to the private parts of a person; my love for a dog and my attraction to human beings to my devotion to God. I would have to find out how these loves worked – did they exclude each other or not. I thought of Judaism in the bar, and the thoughts continued in bed. There had been a time when reality and religion had met in Jewish law and custom. Gradually the marriage had been worn away by time and social change, and now formal religion was restricted to a very narrow and artificial range of human experience. One question followed another. What was the relation between Religion with a big "R", which gave me a scholarship, and religion with a small "r", which was not a business but a love affair, so it could only give me an embrace?

I remembered another line from the Talmud that "a man should not be separated from the community!" I did not want to be separate because my community was home. But I would have to learn the difference between a religious home and a religious prison. There were so many disconnections, but even if they did not seem to relate to each other there were at least three facts: the angels in my soul, my mind with its desire for truth, and the life that flowed in my body. I decided to go back.

I told some friends. One was upset, and said I would regret it. Another told me it was conformism, and another that I was just being sucked back into the class struggle. It was curiously like my exit from the monastery.

In fact everything they said was right, but I was right too, and so I found myself returning to England on the boat train. I wondered what had happened to my linen tabs and velvet hat without the pompom. This amused me – dressing up had never been my line, ecclesiastically or otherwise.

Chapter Fourteen

An honest living

Law, says the priest with a priestly look,
Expounding to an unpriestly people,
Law is the words in my priestly book,
Law is my pulpit and my steeple.

W.H. Auden

What you save from frivolity, add to your
charity.

Rabbi Elijah ben Raphael

The congregation made me very welcome, and for the first
time I think I gave them a real sermon. It was not about what
"the sages said". The last sage I had met (only two days
before, though it seemed a century) was very sage and very
drunk. I had noticed on the Continent how all spirits, human
and divine, produce the same wise platitudes. I ignored the
sages and spoke about what I knew and what I believed. I like
being liked, but I no longer wanted to be just a projection of a
society's needs. I had to try and answer their needs, not just
reflect them. I did not want to revert to childhood and be an
aging good boy for ever. In any case I was not a boy any
longer. Somewhere between my formal Bar Mitzvah and
returning to England I had become a man – though I could
not pinpoint when and where. The congregation liked what I
had to say and, because they liked me, I felt that I had
underrated them. They had come along to synagogue with

personal and real questions, and I could not fob them off with communal or synthetic answers.

On the train back to London I braced myself for all the bumps ahead: my own, and the ones which are implicit in formal religion or in religion on any level.

I would hit the first bump as I came down from the religious high of the service. Time and again this had happened. A part of me had gone ahead of myself, and I enjoyed a few moments, or even a few days, of genuine if fragile sanctity. But I could not keep it up, and when the collapse came I was more irritable than ever. The higher you rise, the lower you fall, and I was no exception to the laws of spiritual gravity. It had happened after the Quaker meeting at Oxford, after the awareness which came with analysis, and after my first months in the Rabbinate. I knew it was going to happen again in the coming week. I had better warn everybody, I thought, to keep out of the way, and let them know what was happening. I was cheered by this. It was the first time I had ever admitted my private fall and taken reasonable precautions for others.

I also realized I should have to cross another religious frontier more often, the one which separates internal from external religion. I could not live – really live – by taking public services, and I did not trust myself to pray by myself. I needed some help and a teacher. It seemed a legitimate thing to pray for, so I prayed for it in the buffet car of the train.

The world I was in was a liberal one, which I liked, but because of that it was more open to the fashions and trends which blew through the suburbs and the middle classes. I needed to recover a little of something older, so that I could occasionally grip the rock of tradition and keep my balance.

Truth seemed to come in many ways. There was the inner truth of experience and feeling and the external truth of form and analysis. There was the truth you discovered yourself, which became part of you, and the truth you learnt from books, which just adhered to you. There were all the masks you had to wear during a day. There was the mask you wore for your boss, and the mask you wore for the person beneath you, and the mask you wore for your own protection or delight. And behind all these masks, was there a real face, or the image of God, or only another mask? I did not know.

On a more practical level I had to sort out the relation of sex and love. Religion, after all, poured out as much about love as any jukebox, but were its counsels any more helpful? It seemed realistic if you made love with one person of the right sex at specified times and possibly in one position. As soon as it moved from this tight situation it got steadily more irrelevant, and sometimes downright silly. There were also the bumps inside the services I was supposed to take, and the prayer books I was supposed to use. Did I have to believe them, and did it matter if I did not?

Then I arrived back in London and after one disconsolate evening, I was quickly drawn back into my old life. I had forgotten how much I had missed it. Having gone away from it, I felt freer to like it for itself and not to criticize it for not being something else.

There were very few Rabbis around, and I quickly got used to being sent round the congregations, a stop gap until something better came down the pipeline.

Like an actor on tour, I learnt a lot from this wandering – not least about myself. After a sermon against superstition, I walked carefully round a ladder without noticing it. Some of the congregation did notice it, and I noticed them, and all of us had some long thoughts. I also learnt, like any actor, that the show has to go on whether you feel like it or not. Sometimes I felt in the mood for prayer, and sometimes I did not or even disliked it. But I had to lead the congregation, and they could not wait for me to etherealize. It did me a lot of good, and I realized that religion was not all inner light and inspired moments. It was also, for example, a business, and I should not despise that aspect of it. Since I accepted payment, at least I could ensure it was good business, not sharp practice, and give fair value.

Though what did value mean in religion? In part, religion is a human toy. People dress up in it, strike postures or attitudes, and it gives us all a stage for acting out our phantasies. Since we can project our prejudices on to the cosmos, it also satisfies the megalomaniac in us. I was one of the toys – a status toy in fact – and there were some good games and funny moments. Some congregations engineered meetings between an orthodox Rabbi and me. Sometimes we disappointed our audience and spoke to each other cordially, at other times we were good entertainment. My orthodox colleague stalked out of the room as I entered it, my nose held haughtily in the air. Everyone was delighted – we had both acted as we should have done. None of this well-meaning ecumenism! A good slanging match with text hurling was "gutsier", especially if you could persuade yourself that you were defending God. If you could, you were released from the Queensberry rules and could kick your opponent below the belt as much as you liked. Modern Israel is a good place to watch this infighting. Jewish religious organizations have just enough power to put some real punch into their disputes and rivalries. You can even persuade yourself sometimes that the struggle is real, which is the test of all good theatre.

It helped me greatly at that time, when I realized that the effective religion of ordinary people was so much nicer than their stated religion. The latter gets logical, and for right reasons thinks up some very appalling things. A saintly, kind and very traditional Rabbi in the nineteenth century wondered if stoning should be reintroduced for adultery. (In Jewish law this would apply more to women who did it less, than to men who did it more.) My congregations knew that something had hastened my adulthood, and no doubt speculated about it. Sometimes they added up two and two and made five, and sometimes they only made three or four. I could not help them because I had not worked out the addition myself.

I left home (it was the right age) and shared some rooms. I have no talent for living alone. A synagogue officer came to see me. He was serious and grim. I was, he stated unnecessarily, living with a man. I was annoyed. The synagogue, I pointed out, did not provide for my company or my house-work. God had created two sexes, and would he prefer me to live with a man or a woman? There was no alternative available in human form, and I could not keep a dog. The grimness turned to a grin, and he suggested we all go out and have a drink – all three of us, he said meaningfully. I asked him if my girl-friend could come too. He agreed with some confusion, and relief. He became angry again when he found she had bobbed blonde hair and was a Methodist who had read Maimonides. It needed two brandies to soothe him, but then you cannot have everything. It served him right too, and I told him so; righteous indignation is such a sleazy emotion. I thought of my sermons, especially the unprepared ones, and resolved never to do likewise.

Chapter Fifteen

"Missing – a Voice!"

I think I have lost something on the way
What it is I do not know.
Shall I turn back? It is so far off now,
Yet it is a pity to let it go.

So I stand still in the midst of the road
Tormented, doubt tossed.
I have lost something, but do not know what
But I know that I've lost.

Abraham Reisen

I got ordained – somehow, somewhere. As I was one of the first graduates of my seminary, no one quite knew what to do; there had been a break in tradition. They made me "Reverend", which I have never been, and gave me a certificate. Then, after a pause, I was made a Rabbi and given another document, handwritten by a Rabbi I liked. I think this was then taken away from me again. I received it once more with a background of organ music, mixed choirs and optimistic blessings. Subsequently this document, to my bewilderment, was replaced by another. It was large, with a big seal and great margins of white. I think I was expected to frame it and hang it over my desk, just as my grandmother hung her marriage contract over her bed to show it was all above-board. It seemed rather blatant, and I let it sink into a mountain of papers and disappear.

There were also some problems about clothes. For some reason "progressive" Jewish ministers wear Roman Catholic hats with pompoms, and as I was supposed to be "conservative" my pompom was vetoed. I was sent to an Anglican outfitter, but I was told to discard the high stiff collar, as it upstaged all my elders and betters. So I wore my tabs tucked into the soft collar of a sports shirt. My stock I have only worn at driving tests, as I was told, inaccurately, that nurses, nuns and ministers were allowed certain indulgences.

During this time I made the usual mistakes and some unusual ones too, as I was "accident-prone" when preaching. I was so eager to be with my congregation in spirit that, carried away by my own words, I walked towards them, stepped over the edge of the pulpit and joined them in the front row. I also fell into a grave, as I threw in the traditional handful of earth. I remember thinking as I went down that it was, thank God, an expensive funeral and the coffin lid would be solid.

I also let the services go on too long, because I wanted to say every word with meaning. Because of my "spirituality" some meals got burnt in ovens. These burnt offerings might be religious, but I knew they were inconsiderate and bad taste in every sense.

The good-nature of Jewish life can easily cope with such capers, and I am pretty sure my congregations egged me on to see what would happen next. A Rabbi has always been trained as the government and police force of a community; he is now expected to entertain his community much more and govern them a lot less.

But I was expected to do something else which frightened me. I felt my communities were asking me to give God back to them. Somewhere on the journey from poverty through persecution to unstable affluence, He had got lost, been shrugged off, pushed off or escaped. For many, their faith had gone up in smoke with the bodies of their parents in the camps. Some had tried to make do with "The Jewish Idea" or "The Spirit of Our History", but you could not fall in love with "Our History" or crack a joke with "The Jewish Idea", so the result was heavy and flat – like stale lumpy bread or Marxist *haute couture*. Most of them did not want a theology – it is an accessory in Judaism not a foundation garment – nor did they want communalism – though that is what they got. They gave dutifully to Israel and felt the normal gut-reactions, but there was a puzzlement about it all. Where was God, and could I through my mysterious and expensive training give Him back to them? My training, as I said, taught me a lot about religion, and I could discourse on it in several living and several dead languages. But for this question I was forced back to the childhood meeting, the angels, animal and human, the love which welled up in the Quaker meeting house, and the door to eternity I saw in the bar in Amsterdam. This was the only capital I had, the only knowledge I knew. It had one characteristic. I had never sought for it, it had just been there or been given. It had little to do with my disappearing diploma.

The problem was easier if we could all start off from where we were and not from where we should be. We were no longer at the centre of our religion, but dwelt on its periphery. We seemed to be insiders of the religious fortress, involved in its work. But the deepest part of ourselves was unconverted, unbelieving and outside. Before the Jewish high holy days, exhausted and irritated by all the organization involved, a leader of my synagogue told me flatly what he did not believe, and it was considerable. I returned doubt for doubt, because I was irritable too. We stared at each other, shaken! He poured out two glasses of neat whisky, an affection sprang up between us, which came from truth as well as booze, and God was with us in our affection. Both of us felt it. We did not doubt quite like that again. The logic of it escapes me; the fact of it I experienced.

One of the strange things about religion is that you can give more than you have, if you know you do not have very much. My chairman and I were both involved with services and prayer books. The books assumed you had "faith", and I was not even clear what that commodity was. It seemed to be a capacity for believing tall stories. Hesitantly I told him my answer. The book was the testimony of past generations – it was the statement of the faith which they had lived on and lived by. It could not be mine (or his) completely. I had an experience of the world my grandparents had never had and, thanks to their hard work, I knew far more. When I prayed, part of me prayed as if I were them, because they were in me, and part of me watched while my faith conversed with their faith. This part did not argue but recognized the similarities, the differences and the same reality which made them bring their prayer books from Russia (their only baggage) and which had got me into the Rabbinate. Time was holy and it moves, and God had placed me in it. I had no "call" to stand still, and neither of us was adjusted to life in a museum of religious antiquities.

The high holy days came to an end and immediately another cycle of festivals succeeded them. With my band of supporters, I prayed my way through those too. I felt as if I was trapped in a liturgical tramline and had blessed God into boredom. Like many children, I used to repeat a word over and over again until it was meaningless. The prayers had gone the same way. Blessing, Blessing, Amen (choral). Stand up, Sit down, Blessing, Amen, Sermon, Stand up, Sit down, Blessing . . . I was pleased when the key to the ark got lost, and was deaf to our prayers (choral) "for God to return to Zion".

Some time later I was going home in the London Underground late at night. Two young people sat opposite me, locked in an embrace which was as passionate as you can get when there is a seat-divider between you. As we clicked our way down the line, she told him he was beautiful and she loved him. He repeated it to her at the next station, and she lobbed the words back at him before we had scarcely moved. A woman in the carriage sighed, looked at them, and sighed again meaningfully at me.

I knew what she meant. It was repetitious and boring, and would never change. Somehow or other, those tired hackneyed words would be as fresh to the lovers at the end of the line as they had been boring for us at its beginning. If you are inside the experience, such repetition is fresh; if you are outside the experience, all words are stale.

I thought of my prayers, and felt a panic. I had been so absorbed in religion that I had lost God. He had fallen into the machine and disappeared. In the confusion of voices and tongues, the voice – my Voice – was just not there. Did I want to recover it, and how could I? Even in a religious magazine you could not put an advertisement: "Missing – a Voice. Return to owner!" I was not, after all, its owner.

Chapter Sixteen

Falling in love with love

Falling in love with love
isn't just make believe.

Popular song

Love the Lord your God with all your
heart . . .

Deuteronomy

Love makes the world go round.

Popular saying

You shall love your neighbour as
you love yourself.

Leviticus

Many years later, I found myself in a small boat, banging a tin tray with a mug in a cotton-wool fog, half-way across the North Sea. At such times I have a tendency to review my life and ask the Almighty why. I knew the reason though, it was love. We had met, had shared a chicken sandwich, and now I was sandwiched between this world and the next.

"Love makes the world go round", and the world hereafter too. Falling in love with God can be very similar to falling in love with a human being. You bump into each other one day, or trip over each other. You meet at a boring formal occasion, like the wedding service of a distant relation – and suddenly you know you want to meet again. Or you realize with wonder that the old familiar God you met years ago in Sunday school classes is alive and attractive (not very different from the boy or girl next door in class B movies). Or you start off by having values and find one day that they are alive. You can speak to them, they can answer back, and you can be in love with them as well as love them. They acquire a human face.

If you are hooked, you start haunting the place where you first met. You want to go to that particular church or synagogue and no other. It takes time to realize that God is everywhere. For although we are formally monotheists, it is easier for us to think and act as dualists. To live and keep sane, we cannot take reality whole, we have to divide it up, though it shows as few seams as the robe of Jesus. It is more convenient for society if one says, this is completely forbidden, that is completely permitted, this worship of God is valid and that form He doesn't care for, that He is present in the liturgy, but not in the loo. In Judaism God might be, is in fact, beyond the categories we have become accustomed to, but to go beyond them and try to find this unification of opposites is a dangerous pastime. It has led to visions and orgies, insight and insanity, saintliness and beastliness. On the other hand if the search is given up or never attempted, the result as I have said is practical dualism. This is less attractive, but an easier option if you have a fearful temperament. It leads to heresy hunts, appropriating God, and a formalism which divides religious experience from actual experience.

Belonging as we do to a legal religion, where one age is ending and another scarcely beginning before our eyes, the second danger is as real for me as the first. It is not however easy to adjust the exact mixture of adventure and boredom that is required. It is a comfort – though a cold one – to know that God's will is done either way – whether we get the proportions right or wrong.

95

In any case, God may be everywhere, but for you at the moment He is localized in a place or an institution. The service takes the place of a guitarist in a café or the cabaret in a night club. At first it is nice to have all the accoutrements of romance around: soft lights, music, candles – what more could you want? Even the sermon might turn you on – in love anything can happen, certainly at the beginning.

There will be moments of course when you will want to be alone. This is as difficult in religion as it is in ordinary life. In Protestant churches the doors are firmly shut and you cannot ask the caretaker for the key – he will feel suspicious, and you will feel illicit. Catholic churches and synagogues may also be barred, because the more people drop in, the more the insurance they have to pay. (The Lord of Hosts is as imprisoned by His possessions as any suburban couple.) Some groups dedicated to silence, like the Quakers, have a meditation room, but it is hard to find and feels empty like a pub outside normal hours. Curiously enough the highest percentage of locked churches I have found is in Spain. Even the temples you do get into are not always suitable. Sometimes they are cathedrals, and having a private talk with God in them is like trying to have an intimate chat in a department store.

Sooner or later the crisis will come, and you will have to take Him (or Her) back to your place. It is difficult because the Holy One does not fit your furniture or your books. If you are a Jew you will have to re-arrange your kitchen for example. As in any love affair you will have to make room for Him inside yourself as well, in your heart.

It is not easy sharing a kitchen with anybody, and it is even less easy sharing yourself with another being. After the first rapture, there is the adjustment period when you both have to learn to live together. It can be very irritating. He wants to go to Mass and you want to go sailing. You would like a ham rasher or a battery chicken, and He says He could not stand it. If the love and commitment are strong you can overcome the gap, and like many couples you will gradually get more alike, and one day you may fuse together.

Of course there will be rows. You can tell Him to get out of your life, and He will go. But after love has gone, you will feel so empty, you will call Him back. There is nothing like the pleasure of making up. It usually leads to a release of love. With a human being, it is consummated in bed, and with a divine being, in repentance. Lovers' quarrels are well known, and the pattern can be repeated many times. But take care! After one quarrel He may leave you. You will wait for His return, and for the normal reconciliation. But He has his own will and own thoughts, and He may not return. Then you will have to live with the emptiness like any forsaken lover, when the colour drains out of the world and a dimension of it is lost and love is a memory.

At this time in my life I started dropping into places where I could pray: synagogues, churches and temples. After some hesitation, I found myself talking to God, usually asking Him what I should do next. I did not go in for thanks or praise, because at that time I did not think I had much to give thanks for. Nor did I find myself asking for forgiveness. My life had been chaotic, and a lot of it was not my fault. Whether He forgave me was His own business, whether I forgave Him or myself was mine.

I also had to work out if our love was exclusive or not. Did the love of God rule out the other loves of my life? Was He in fact jealous? With some people it does not seem that the relationship is like that. I increasingly came to see Him not as a rival to other loves but as part of them. I looked into someone else's face with love, and found Him present. He in fact showed me what love looks like – its true face.

Having said all this, I give the cautions you need after a religious experience. You might intend to embrace the universe, but you can end up just giving yourself a hug or admiring your own spirituality, or kissing your own ego.

Chapter Seventeen

Cautions on religious experience

Margaret Fuller: I accept the universe.
Carlyle: Gad! She'd better!

The cautions which follow are the result of my own experience of religious experience. Although these problems affected me in a very personal way, they are general. It helps me to use the second person, not the first person, when describing them, as I was left rather bruised from it all. By this polite fiction I can be more precise and detached about something which attached me.

The first danger in religious experience is that you will get high on it. The experience part will overshadow the religious part. Since the problem which religious experience tries to solve is hedonism, it does not help you if you make your hedonism cosmic. Religious experience is then in conflict with real religion. This is why dry periods have to come and why they are necessary.

Another caution. There is little point in asking whether the kind of interior conversation I have described is inner or outer. It is neither, or it is both. Often the inner voice can fasten on some external form or object. With me it is a candle or an eternal light, for Christians it can often be a statue or an image. It is very important to realize that these are only the clothes of the religious reality, the packaging, so to speak; they are not the reality itself. You must keep this "as if" quality in mind or the statue or image will become a doll and you will

98

end up by playing children's games, wanting to dress it up and put it to bed. Religious experience should make you childlike: it should not make you childish.

If you have just got into the "God business", you may be so surprised that anything happens at all in prayer that you will become over-possessive. It will become your own too much. You will forget that you only understand it in part. Just because an experience is mystical, it does not withdraw you from the class struggle. The genuine experience is quite capable of standing up to analysis or criticism. You might have to be protected; it does not.

There is another trap which seems so obvious that you may not notice the danger. Some part of your mind will reason like this "I come from a certain environment, and I have had a genuine perception or revelation or insight or what-have-you. Therefore, in order to have the same perception or revelation or insight or what-have-you, another person must have the same background as me and share my attitudes." This simple misunderstanding is at the root of most religious fanaticism. The experience will not open the mind to new awareness and make it bigger, it will merely cut the cosmos down to your size and make infinity parochial. The *mysterium tremendum* will take on all the limitations of provincial Ireland or Jewish suburbia. This is what has taken place in Northern Ireland and the Middle East.

The experience will also be surrounded by a fuzz of neurosis, or it may even work through your neuroses. In any case it will not be aseptic and uncontaminated. Therefore it will require several levels of understanding, because it contains several layers of meaning. The same criteria apply to religious states as to scientific statements: "By their fruits you shall know them." If the fruits lead to escapism – to the religious equivalent of "as the sun sinks slowly in the west" – then be careful. If they lead you back to your pots and pans and typewriters and your account books and daily life they are more reliable.

It may be right and necessary to think of God as a person for prayer to work, but in doing so, do not forget the "as if" element and start playing off this "person" against such very mundane persons as a husband or a wife. Religion can be used then to enjoy what can only be called a spiritual adultery. Unlike more earthy affairs, the other human partner will be unable to defend herself or himself. You cannot compete with a ghost, especially a holy one, for romance and sensation.

One of the great difficulties will be holding on to what you have actually experienced and what you have actually learnt. The pressure to distort or deny comes from all directions, some of them unexpected. Firstly people will tell you that your experience is only subjective (though what experience is not?) and, as if it follows automatically, that it is just illusion. You have to realize that prayer and spirituality, which seem so harmless, are profoundly disturbing for many people. They may seem solicitous for your peace of mind, but it is their own selves they are really coddling. Since they have not trusted their own experience, or risked their own adventure into prayer, they probably are not aware of the comfort and internal criticism it contains. Anyway it is going to be difficult to hold on to what you have actually known.

The attack will also come from the opposite direction: from the devout, from the media and from yourself. They will want you to inflate your experience, to give it greater "body", though it has no body, as you know. You will also feel that it is pretty unsubstantial, so you will not be averse to a little tarting-up. A bit of technicolour goes down well at cocktail parties. Provided you do not deceive yourself it probably does not much matter; it is after all "as if" stuff, but you might fall into the trap which always appears whenever you and truth part company. You will get into trouble in the end because you will not be able to distinguish what happened and what you made up, and therefore will not believe in any of it.

Another problem comes from a more unexpected source –

the religious institution. There really is a problem here. If you have your own hot-line to God, and the institution has its own hot-line through tradition, the result may be holy schizophrenia. Usually, if you do not agonize over it too much, it will sort itself out. After all, Freudians, Jungians and Adlerians have had to compromise with each other. So do capitalists and Marxists, and they are all part of the same cosmos. Of course if you are coming from a secular position like me, you will not have the same attitude to tradition as a cloistered nun, and you can only evaluate it in the light of your own experience. For religious people, the holy text is the tradition and their lives are a kind of commentary around it. But for the secular person coming to religion, it is very much the other way around. Your life, your experience, is the text and the tradition is the commentary helping you to understand your life. Many religious people have gone ahead of themselves. They are insecure and therefore can feel more threatened by religious experience than any other group. I have attended many retreats for professionals and for laymen. The former are always the most difficult for me. Religious experience never quite fits. It is a free element and therefore creates problems for anyone trying to run something. It is a creative and anarchic element in an ordered structure. Literary critics must have the same problem with writers or poets, and art dealers with the painters they handle. People get too frightened, but traditional religion could not have survived changing times and cultures unless it had found some door within itself which could be open to freshness and the spirit.

These are I think general problems of religious experience. There are other consequences which may be purely personal. One of the most unexpected effects of prayer was for me the gift of laughter. Life seemed lighter, more buoyant. Perhaps it was because I trusted it a little more, did not fight it and could flow along with it.

Another unexpected side-effect was that I became more difficult to live with. This occurred especially after retreats. I suppose it was because I was working on two levels, and was, as a result, more inconsistent and more puzzling to others around me and to myself. A moment of grace had come, but I just could not keep it, could not hold it, so I felt sad, for I had lost something. I could not acquire it or buy it, I had to wait for it in patience.

When I was at Oxford I read the parables of the kingdom of heaven. Walking down the street, chairing a meeting or smoking in bed, I found the kingdom of heaven occasionally opened to me. I did not pray; I was in prayer. It was not something to strive for; it was something to accept. I also stepped out of the kingdom just as surely and involuntarily as I had entered into it. I was not ready to live in it. I was still only a day tripper into it on a tourist's visa.

Chapter Eighteen

The facts of life

Bring us the little foxes,
    the foxes, who destroy the vineyards,
for our vineyards are in blossom
    and our vines have tender grapes.

Song of Songs

If love depends on some selfish cause, when
the cause disappears love disappears, but if
love does not depend on a selfish cause it will
never disappear. What love depended on a
selfish cause? Amnon's love for Tamar (2 Samuel 13).
What love did not depend on a selfish cause?
David's love for Jonathan (1 Samuel 18).

Sayings of the Fathers (Talmud)

With my body, I thee worship.

Anglican Marriage Service

The experience of many worlds has made me a good compromiser, and I long ago gave up the pursuit of ideological tidiness. This has stood me in good stead because by some quirk of fate I no longer stand in a pulpit and discourse on the general rules, extolling the purity of faith, the sanctity of the family, and a tradition which can supply an answer to every question. Instead I sit in an office and try to clear up the débris when the rules break down, and deal with the situations which were never supposed to happen – the Jewish boy who fell in love with the gentile girl next door, or the bitterness which underlies the bland statements in civil divorce documents. My stated work is to formalize such situations and resolve them in the context of Jewish tradition, as far as I can. I do my best, and I tie a knot here and a knot there, linking my religion to reality. But I cannot do very much, as the separation is now very wide, and it will be a long time before the two come together again. In the meantime, I must admit my ignorance, and go back to learn from life, like any artist after an academic education.

In some way or other the problems of my work centre round the diseases and illnesses of religious love. These are not confined to bed or business, but also spoil my breakfast as well. For example, most mornings in the post I get an assorted mixture of religious tracts, journals and texts. I put them aside; occasionally out of curiosity I read them through. It is a strange cocktail for breakfast time – lumpy with love and looniness. The effect is disturbing, as underneath the love in some there is quite a lot of sadism. There is a lot of concern, a lot of meanness, and it is all laced with emotional blackmail. I am bribed with heavens I do not wish to enter, threatened by hells which come out of toasted cheese and nightmares, and my soul is loved but the other parts of me are not even liked. Such love may be permissible in the higher regions of religions, but it would not be acceptable for a moment on the lower levels of marriage guidance.

I am not sure why this illness exists. Perhaps it is because the sexual component of love has been ignored or suppressed. The stylized and sexless falsetto of many religious services is an example. One Christian lady was, I am told, asked in a survey if heaven existed. "Yes," she answered. "What would it be like?" the interviewer asked. "Just like this world, without sex," she replied. Even in my own tradition, which is freer, I do not think women of my grandmother's generation got much joy from one part of their marriage. Some were worn out by child-bearing, creeping to Marie Stopes' Clinic in fear of their husbands, and played on sexually, as if they were objects like cellos or violins. I do not think their needs were ever really understood or satisfied. It is good that such injustices have gone. It is a pity the godly passed them by and atheists and agnostics and a few fringe religious people came to their help.

Perhaps the infection of religious love came because it was once entangled with property, ownership and jealousy, and never really got disentangled from them. The Pentateuch for example does not mention marriage, but says, "if a man acquires a woman". I watch the result of all this "acquiring" in my work, people trying to capture each other, or fighting for the freehold of each other (though it is more realistic to call it the leasehold now).

A theological problem is connected with this jealousy. Religious people often love their own in a destructive way. Orthodox people feel more orthodox by being rude to liberals (and vice-versa). Catholics feel more catholic by patronizing Anglicans, and Anglicans do the same to the Free Churches (and vice-versa).

Since my student days more changes have occurred, and the gap between formal religion and reality has widened still further, as the link between sexuality and procreation has weakened. In Catholicism this produced a crisis of religious authority; in all religions it meant that sexuality has to be considered straightforwardly as pleasure, without a covering of purpose, usefulness or biology. In the past, religion has felt uncomfortable about pleasure; it has traditionally used pain, sorrow or guilt to provide the energy for spiritual ascent. Its classic stories depend on situations of deprivation or poverty, not on affluence and satisfaction.

In this situation it is not so easy to know what sins are, to see the real ones, not just the formal ones which you can look up in the index. To spot them in fact you need religious awareness and sensitivity. You also need spirituality to cope with them. For example, the holy spirit is often needed to carry on sleeping with someone after orgasm has taken place. A deep sensitivity is required to say "no" graciously to an advance, especially from an old or handicapped person (provided of course you want to say no). It is easy to use religion to reinforce one's own concrete virtue by slapping someone else in the face. To accept the sexual needs of another person (emotional, physical and technical) requires a listening as profound as that required by prayer. An old Rabbi once told me that religion was "giving without strings". Sexuality can be cruel, ruthless and selfish. With a little help from the soul, it can be transformed. The gap between human sexuality and divine love is not so great as many like to think. A sex shop opened near a place where I worked. It had hooked truncheon-like objects, sensitizers and other articles, for which my experience and imagination are too restricted. Earnest couples came in, gravely studied them, and compared them for utility and price. I wandered round absorbed and wondering, and then started giggling. I abruptly stopped, as I remembered that I was subject to the same giggles in shops and repositories for equally bizarre objects of piety; both are unintentionally funny. Whether divine or human, it did not seem to affect my reactions.

A second change has affected the roles of the sexes. They are no longer fixed, and increasingly each couple is working out its own balance of functions and duties. This concerns washing-up, cooking, sexual positions, and is beginning to affect religious ritual too. A man can do the washing-up, and a woman does not always have to look up at the ceiling. There is more experiment, more variety and more understanding and generosity.

A third change concerns the needs of minorities. All communities and societies are tested by their treatment of their own minorities – not just other people's minorities. "Remember you were slaves in the land of Egypt." All of them however concentrate on the times they were oppressed, not on the times when they were oppressors. A spiritual advance takes place when a religious group can acknowledge itself as a persecutor and not see itself only among the persecuted.

Homosexuals and lesbians are a good example of groups whose needs have scarcely been acknowledged or understood. Their number is constant, and their contribution to religion has been significant if unacknowledged. Since they cannot rely on social connections to deepen their relationships or stabilize them, they have had to find more strength in themselves. Precisely because they cannot use social props, there is often an inner search which touches a deep inner reality and truth. Unfortunately they have been considered "outsiders", so those who need spirituality are precisely those who are put off by it.

They are one example of a great problem. Religion has a habit of telling you where you ought to be and not starting from where you are. It is also not very good at telling you how to get from one to the other, or how to value the experiences *en route*. If you are a man who is attracted to men or a woman who is attracted to women, it makes little sense to hear that Natural Law forbids it and that what you fancy you naturally feel is technically unnatural. Another example concerns young people. The age of the greatest sexual desire and the age of marriage or committed relationships are now separated. Some people prefer not to experiment in the intervening period; an increasing number do. You cannot simulate the commitment of a marriage, but you can learn a lot about yourself in a relationship. It depends a great deal on your needs, your scruples, your ability to direct sexual energy into other channels. Such experiments, such liaisons, are without benefit of clergy no matter how well-meaning or serious. But short does not always mean shallow.

Judaism has journeyed from polygamy and concubinage to strict monogamy, but another change is taking place, barely disguised by quick divorce. The new situation will also need to be sanctified.

Nearly two thousand years ago there was a battle about the Song of Songs. Should it go into the Bible or not? It scarcely mentions God, it talks about love and sex but not about marriage, and it uses an erotic terminology based on the symbolism of the vineyard. According to Rabbinic story, it had to be rescued from the house of feasting and of wine: ie, a tavern or a night club. Many Rabbis were against its inclusion, but Rabbi Akiba was for, and it got in. It is the basis of the Zohar, the classic of Jewish mysticism, and also the basis of St John of the Cross's poems. I doubt if any religious group would have the courage to include it today.

Chapter Nineteen

Olde-tyme religion

I want ole time religion
I want ole time religion
It was good enough for pappy
and it's good enough for me

Revivalist song

The clock outside my brain moves on, the clock inside it stands still. Being young for me still means crew cuts, white socks and looking like a fresh clean-living American kid. After some years in the Rabbinate, I had to go to youth conferences again, and teach students, some of whom I had taught or confirmed many years before but now met again at conferences and at colleges.

I was startled by their looks. Chestnut curls draped their shoulders, the boys looked like Jesus and the girls rather droopy. Each wave of ideology had left a thin residue – Provo, hippie and flower power. I suppose it was the last which had wiped away the baseball eagerness and replaced it by droopy concern.

I was even more startled by the religious knick-knacks they wore, and one young man made me think of a Jewish Christmas tree, if such things exist. The men wore skull caps, which were very small like postage stamps (small is beautiful and pious as far as skull caps are concerned). Great tassels hung out of their trousers, strong enough to pull curtains as well as being reminders of God. One listener also wore a "gartel", a kind of belt which separated his higher from his lower centres. I wondered if it still worked.

I had not seen the like since my childhood. If this was the future, it looked too much like the past. So was my journey from the warm darkness of tradition to enlightenment and biblical criticism and dry martinis really necessary?

I got even more confused when I found the Christians I knew travelling equally determinedly to the future in contrasting apparel. The nuns were getting rid of their robes and wimples, and as fast as they were getting rid of them the same garments were being snapped up by youngsters in a trendy street market. One sister told me she only kept her habit to oblige Jewish friends, who needed her for marches and demonstrations.

The confusion was ecumenical and total. Some young Jews, jaded by progress, asked a monk to help them with a retreat. "Do not retreat," said the monk, "It is a dirty word; go forward instead, and progress to social concern." "We have already done that," said the Jews. So they parted company, each one to do his thing.

My thing was God, and I decided it was a good idea to do it more and get better acquainted with Him before my religion turned into social slumming too. Unlike my students I decided against chestnut curls or, in my case, grizzled locks. I was also too far gone for a "gartel" to be effective. Nevertheless they were on the right trail, and I too needed a dose of traditional religion. I did not mind very much about the flavour but I did want the real thing, "olde-tyme" if necessary, but genuine. The packaging is so good these days that you can easily be fooled and, as I have said before, be taken for a ride instead of a trip to heaven.

It is not easy to find the real thing. There are for example a lot of gurus and swamis around, and their names look very impressive until you realize that some of them have not got a name at all. It is just a mass of titles like "saint", "divine" and "holiness". You do not spot it because you do not know the culture behind it and cannot have a feel about what is profound and what is trendy. There are also traditional groups in Judaism and Christianity who increase their "efficiency" by playing with the media. For me, the media have subtly but definitely affected their message. Perhaps they know it, perhaps they do not. If you use a loudspeaker, you cannot help going in for simplifications, and you certainly cannot get personal in a modern auditorium. You can try, but concern *en masse* always seems phony to me. The general answer is very close to being a private irrelevance, or even a lie.

I have said that I did not care too much about which variety or "flavour" of traditional religion, and this needs some explanation. For some reason which I do not understand, medieval religious attitudes died in Europe in the horror of the last war. Christian groups try to love Jews now, rather than to convert them. Though a few may cross the religious frontiers in either direction (often for marriage), for most such formal side movements across the ecumenical "chessboard" are irrelevant to their religious progress. Christianity after all nearly conquered the world by the end of the nineteenth century, but neither Christianity nor the world changed that much.

As conversion has died down and the numbers game with it, religious groups grab less from each other but learn more. I have travelled through most shades of Judaism, and my journey (I hope) has not ended yet. The generation which followed me was even more adventurous and experimented with many more cults and philosophies. I do not think it occurs to young Jews any more that such a journey is in conflict with their Judaism.

For myself, I have been strongly attracted to Vedanta because of its clarity and precision. Mentally it is the most satisfying philosophy, but I cannot use it because I need a personal God for devotion, garnished with angels if possible.

111

Christianity on the other hand is satisfying for devotion, but not possible for belief. And Judaism – well, it is where the God of my fathers put me and it is home. . . . Being a convert solves certain problems; not being a convert solves even more.

Because the religious tug of war has stopped – two rival concerns battling for the concession of an individual soul – we can now begin to learn from each other, bringing home the lessons and integrating them with care into our own background. This integration is already taking place. It is not blessed by the powers that be, though the Power above seems to prosper it. Despite all the fears of syncretism, people do not just stay put in their religious homes: they take religious journeys, they go on a pilgrimage, they take time off and go on spiritual holidays – free-range or packaged. Only an insensitive or a stupid man would be completely unaffected by it all, learning nothing and bringing back no souvenir.

In the post-holocaust period, most Jews treated the word "assimilation" as if it were a dirty word. They preferred to think of their religion as autonomous. Yet orthodox synagogues have much in common with Orthodox churches, in attitude as well as in style. Reformed and liberal synagogues have the same link with reformed churches and liberal Christian theology. In Israel, the influence of Islam on Judaism is strong, though unacknowledged by either side.

Many Christians wander into Judaism to complete their Christianity. New services are coming into existence linking the Passover and the Eucharist. The new styles of communion look much more like the Jewish Kiddush which was its origin.

This is just one symptom of a process which is growing if unauthorized. It is also not confined to religious institutions and traditions. The give-and-take extends to the secular world too. The Jewish world can cope with it because of its cultural and communal cocoon. The Christian world, which has more belief than culture, will have to resolve it on a profounder level. The cosmic Christ was known to the early Church, but the Hindu contact has given it a body and relevance it would otherwise not possess. If you think of course that your own brand has all truth in its best form, these comments will be irrelevant.

I was therefore open to religious adventure, whether it came via a Khanka, a monastery or a Yeshivah. It was the depth I was concerned with not the flavour. The theology I could also work out for myself if it bothered me (actually it does not).

I needed old-fashioned religion, because it faces the right way. It is centred on what God needs, and not what a human being wants. There is a conflict of wills in religion. It does not exclude humour, and it does not have to be tragic, but it is there and I know it. It can be greeted with a laugh or with tears, but as the Talmud says; "without our consent we are born, without our consent we die, and without our consent we are forced to a judgment." In *The Brothers Karamazov*, the distance between the Grand Inquisitor and Christ is tragic. In the Rabbinic story of Rabbi Eliezer's excommunication, it is rueful and funny. But the same gap, the distance between human and divine, is there. It does not change, and much religion is concerned with giving up protests and accepting the reality. How you wish to do this is your own business, provided you do it – with guitars or in silence, alone or in company, smiling bravely or bursting into tears.

I also needed a place which catered for prayer and not for services; in which if a still small voice spoke, I could at least hear it (whether I followed it was another matter). In theory I could do it in the park across the road from where I live; in practice I like other people doing the same thing or a similar thing together with me. An hour of silence is disturbing. People who tell you there is nothing in the silence seem to find a remarkable number of reasons why they themselves and others prefer not to risk it.

I wanted to get away from the rat-race as well for a time. The distortion it produces is everywhere. All people may be equal in the love of God, but they are not in the calculations of their fellow human beings. In a bar or night club the distortion comes from sex or money. In a religious or political institution it comes from position, status or ambition, and possibly from money as well. It is there of course in a contemplative set-up too, but if it is genuine and of reasonable antiquity, there are more safeguards.

It is good if the place is unfamiliar and a bit frightening. We make ourselves as comfortable as we can, but the universe is not a cosy place and it is worthwhile practising giving up or dying to ourselves before we give up everything and die to everything except the voice in the silence. The experience can be reassuring, and we learn not to be afraid of the dark.

I also wanted to be with people who had prayed a lot. People get as romantic about religion as they do about love. Prayer is work, it requires practice and practice makes perfect – sometimes – as in everything else. People who pray seriously interest me. They have a quality I want to share, and they hear and see things that I pass over. Their language fits what I experience, and so I trust it.

I have recommended the searchers I know to find a place where they can stand aside from their ordinary lives to see what is extraordinary in it. Some go to Jewish Yeshivahs, some to Hindu Ashrams, and some to Sufi Khankas. I have a great affection for a contemplative priory. It is genuine, nobody is trying to sell me anything, I can get on with my own thing, and it is on the motorway which passes near my house. They are vegetarian too, which solves my Kashrus problem. Could a Jewish Rabbi ask for more?

Chapter Twenty

"Get thee to a nunnery"

*Some cautions for visitors to traditional
religious establishments (Ashrams, Monasteries,
Yeshivahs, etc.)*

I've often thought I'd like to join a monastery. But then
I'd have to behave myself much more than I'm able to do.
                                              Gilbert Harding

The poor darlings (the Jews). I'm awfully fond of
them, and I'm awfully sorry for them, but it's their own
silly fault – they ought to have let God alone.
                                              Hilaire Belloc

I do not use the term "olde-tyme" scathingly or whimsically.
Although most people cannot live within the old traditional
structures, they cannot live without them either, because the
enlightenment has not produced (yet) its own patterns of piety
and devotion. The breadth is there, and much depth, but it
remains individual, it has not been worked into a system.
Sooner or later you will want or need a dose of olde-tyme
religion in Jewish, Christian or other flavours. You will want
to pack your bags and retreat to a monastery, a nunnery, a
Yeshivah or a Khanka, or something similar.

There will be a number of misunderstandings, and it is
better to face them at the beginning. As a Jewish patron of
such establishments, who gets great benefit from them (in-

deed they are essential), I have tripped up many times.

You will be using the spirituality to live in the world, while the avowed purpose of the set-up may be to help you die to the world, or be at least impervious to it. You may not be prepared to die just yet. (A curious feature of monasteries is the bravery in facing major illnesses and the worry and attention paid to minor ones, usually stomach, sinus and psychosomatic worries which do not fit their view of life.)

You will be thinking in terms of a short stay (with breaks to scamper back to girl-friends and normalcy) – they might be thinking of your stay as a try-out for eternity. Unless you get a superior with unusually superior understanding you are in trouble. (Perhaps I was lucky, but the ones I met had it.)

There is a great difference between an affair and a marriage, and the former cannot be a trial run for the latter. You cannot simulate commitment. The real effect comes when you hear the doors closing behind you for good.

You wanted old-tyme religion, so do not complain if you have got it. You may have to put up with board beds, bells, bleeding hearts, jokes which are too weak, tea which is too strong and fish which is too high. The most difficult thing will not however be the food, it will be obedience. Should you be obedient when you really disagree (real absurdity is known now and guarded against)? On the one hand you will not get much further in the "destruction of the ego" unless you can accept it – on the other hand, it was the sincere defence of Eichmann too, and you know what that led to. Be obedient, but be very careful whom you choose to be obedient to! (Do not forget that it is your choice, and do not try to evade the responsibility.)

There are certain inconvenient sciences – not physics, chemistry or mathematics, but history, textual criticism and a lot of psychology and sociology. Be prepared to think "olde-tyme" at least for a while. You can sort it all out later.

Do not let any of this put you off. You do take a risk. You

can never tell where you will end up, once you are launched into religious waters and start having intimate chats with the cosmos. But you can face that when and if it ever arises. Above all, do not start improving on the work of the Almighty and, if you are Christian for example, adding your own plastic crosses to His real ones.

Religious institutions try to be, but are not, free from empire-building, (the crusades were an old form of it), and you will have to prevent yourself becoming another addition to the convert intake. It does not do you or them any good, unless it is real.

All the above are fairly common to most knockers at the doors of religious establishments. Some are my own hang-ups, though I think they are all fairly general.

It is worth soldiering on even if it does seem a bit gloomy, or restrictive. The freedom is in the prayers, the space in the great vistas within you, and you learn to see the things you get when you give up and the unsuspected lights that shine in darkness.

Chapter Twenty-one

The religion in Religion

As the Day of Atonement service was about to commence, the Rabbi had an idea. He raised his hand, and in the presence of the congregation approached the ark, opened it, and prostrated himself before it. "Lord," he said, "I am but dust and ashes." Before the Rabbi could return to his seat, the Cantor too raised his hand, opened the ark again, and prostrated himself before it. "Lord," he said, "I too am but dust and ashes." Before he could commence the service, the beadle raised his hand, approached the ark, opened it, and prostrated himself before it. "Lord," he said, "Also I am but dust and ashes."

"Look," the Rabbi said to the Cantor, "who thinks he is only dust and ashes!"

Jewish joke

When I was a Rabbinic student, I was sent to a small congregation outside London, and I day-dreamed romantically and happily. I would come back to it and serve my flock for years and years and years (it never occurred to me that they would get as bored with me as I would with them). I would be wise and humble and unnoticed, except by God of course, and some religious cognoscenti. My hair would grow grey in their service, and my sermons ripen like old Stilton; I would be rather holy.

It did not work out like that. Jewish congregations are not flocks, and I have called synagogue councils many names, some very affectionate, some aggressive, but "sheep" is the last word I should apply to them – thank God. The situation did not require a young Bing Crosby playing at being a Jewish Rabbi, and there were so few of us at the time that I had to try my hand at everything.

For a while I had a long title and little money. I was "in charge" of Europe and felt like the bishop of a bankrupt diocese. I was sent to America to lecture and collect what funds I could, if I could. So instead of ripening like old Stilton in the country, I was eating it washed down with Bourbon at the Los Angeles Hilton. I trotted around Geneva and Rome, feeling ecumenical and jet-set, and was invited to a highball in the Vatican bar.

The technology of religion fascinated me – the pressured fund-raising, the fast committees where you could hear the minds of ecclesiastics buzzing away like computers, the generosity, the alcohol, the kindness and the name-dropping. I wandered happily from synagogue to synagogue and from church to church, blessing kings, queens, crown princes and presidents in every language I knew, and some I didn't. One synagogue had a pulpit which rose in the air electronically and unexpectedly, leaving me like a monkey on a stick. In another the lights turned blue as I got to the memorial prayers. In yet another, where I was invited by the chairman or president, the Rabbi informed me in a hoarse whisper as I was about to begin, that I had stolen his pulpit. It was all good clean fun, and for the greater glory of God.

My first reaction was covert enjoyment, and overt dis-approval. Organization was worldly and bad, spirituality romantic and good. I felt someone ought to take me away from all this. My dislike of organization quickly turned to respect and then to admiration. I was shown around the offices of the Common Market and only wished I knew how to recruit kindness and goodness in the way those offices knew how to deal with industry. A manufacturer showed me a vast computer, and I wondered if religion must always be vague and evasive. Could it never achieve that clean precision? I decided I had not looked into machines enough. The wisdom, the experience, the technology and the discipline which go into an aircraft engine are truly marvellous. It takes so much to send it up, and one unresolved childhood aggression to crash the marvel down.

While I was thinking about all this, my attitude to inner religion changed. I no longer thought of it as the cherry on the cake, the *de luxe* extra, the trading stamps given away with the goods, but as a vital component of my job, its dynamic, its source of vitality. Without the awareness of God, Rabbis changed subtly but surely into communal executives, and synagogues changed into country clubs. Judaism itself became a vast "auld lang syne" society mumbling about its memories and its crumbling folk culture, its aches and its identity problems. Without God, it was not worth the death of six million. It was not worth the death of one. I certainly would not give up my life for nostalgia.

In any case, without the awareness of God religion could only be politics and bad politics too, because it did not have a really political aim – only survival or expediency. There was nothing wrong with committees and organization, provided they were not autonomous but led to and worked for something else which was not another committee or another organization. There was nothing wrong in jet-setting to Geneva either, provided you knew Whom you were doing it for. Unless you did, it would all get very boring, like a committee which has ceased to deal with its proper work but has got sidetracked instead into the ego problems of its members.

Organized Religion is not religion itself, but it is a powerful stimulant to it. If you do decide to go into it, it is better to dive right in than to wander round the edges of the pool, putting in a toe and complaining the water is too cold. Once you are in, really in, you are forced to go deeper, or you lose your self respect or your soul. If you are a professional the choice becomes clear and stark quite quickly. Are you doing what is right or what is expedient? Are you preaching what is fashionable or what is true? Are you more frightened of God or of your employers? I like Organized Religion. It does not solve any religious problem by itself, but you are forced to get to the point of the problem quicker without wasting so much time.

I also needed inner religion more, to help me see the obvious. If you are a Rabbi, you can end up thinking that everybody is a young married couple belonging to a mortgaged middle class. You can also think that the whole world is the Jewish problem. You need God to see Palestinian refugees, the mixed marriages, the sexual and economic minorities and all the outsiders in an insider's world. Unless you pray hard, you just don't see them, though they are there in front of your eyes.

I also needed God so that I could walk alone when I had to. I am a gregarious person, belonging to a gregarious religion. The danger of the set-up is conformity and looking over one's shoulders. Unless you pray it through, the set-up itself can become your God, or you and your colleagues become each other's gods. Idols and images are not problems any longer, but community self-worship is their modern equivalent. Every religious tradition has its special virtue, and wedded to its special virtue is its special temptation. My own religion approaches divinity through law, custom and community. When divinity is ditched (the reason does not matter), law and custom become autonomous, rather like tabus. Community ceases to be the expression of worship and becomes its object. When their inner balance is disturbed legal religions like Judaism (and possibly Islam) slide into communalism and politics. Christianity seems to have a different danger. It is more individual, more linked to private feeling and experience. When it goes astray, happenings do not lead to experience, they replace it. The result is not unlike a pop festival – pop goes integrity! Priests, laymen and religious are with it, but what "it" is, God alone knows.

An even more important reason for spirituality came from the requirements of my job. I did not feel I had to prophesy, but I had to do something quite like it. I had to try and see what was happening under the surface of events, what was the real problem behind the publicized and stated problems. Every minister knows that when someone comes to him with a religious problem, there is always something behind it which has been left out consciously or unconsciously. It is the same with communal problems and events. Behind the political reality there is a metaphysical reality. But you need a lot of silence before you can point your finger at it. The early 'sixties were boom time. We had "never had it so good". It was quite obvious though that a wave of violence was coming, because people – young people especially – do not live by bread alone but by myths as well. I was introduced to the President of Germany and told him. He listened politely, and I got a nice dinner. He got 1968 and student revolt instead.

Sitting on trains, or delayed in airports, or waiting for Godot or for my ship to come in, I decided to broaden my religious education and not waste time flitting from the bar to the duty-free with *Time Magazine*. From my wartime days, I still had a prejudice against religious literature, and rather reluctantly and indiscriminately started to buy some spiritual paperbacks. I was not prepared for hardback editions yet. I was not sure the contents would have that much use, and their covers that much wear.

Chapter Twenty-two

Wisdom while waiting

Saint Monica
Is not my favourite saint
Moral blackmail
Is not an attractive taint.

Monica Furlong

If you get to heaven
    before I do
Just bore a hole
    and pull me through!

Student song

Become the writing and the meaning yourself!

Angelus Silesius

Many years ago Henry Miller wrote an article about the great
books which had never influenced him: I think Shakespeare
was at the top. When I began my religious education for
myself, I had difficulties with the great books of my own
religion and the Scriptures of other faiths as well. Firstly, the
events they described were too long ago and you needed a
mountain of scholarship to relate them to your own life. I
flicked open an Old Testament and hit a stirring denunciation
of Edom. The cultural shock was too great, and I proceeded
to the New. Somewhere in the Acts of the Apostles there is a
story about some waverers or half-hearted religious people

being struck down dead. As I have always been a stumbler and doubter, if not a waverer, I hastily shut it and decided to try something else instead. The Scriptures are the basis of it all, but at first glance they are neither nice nor relevant; I thought I would prefer them predigested. Lots of people starting off on a religious search get turned off in this way. The second problem about the Bible and the Talmud was that I had learnt them for an examination, not for their own sake, so that I was not fresh enough for them. They would therefore have to come at the end of my reading list, not at the beginning. The third reason was that they were bulky and I could not carry them around with me. I felt guilty, but cheating is no use with God, even for the most pious reasons – it is like cheating yourself.

A lot of modern theology passed me by as well. It seemed to tell you how you could believe in something, if you did not believe it. Most of the problems seemed to come from a confusion of truths, mythological and historical, inner and outer, communal and personal. For some people it is important to put each statement in its pigeonhole. For me this is not a useful pastime as the world is too untidy, and I do not think it gets you very far.

I was more interested in the underworld of religious piety – the partisan magazines which most devout groups issue to their followers. A lot of the contents are irrelevant if you are an outsider, but occasionally there is something so true, so personal and so artless that it hits home. I found myself more and more interested in religious people and what they had made of the signs of God's presence in their lives.

Some religious literature disturbed me because, though the words were love, the taste was hate. Some of the faiths were quite nasty about each other, some only condescending, very few tried to understand what another religion looked like from inside. There was a lot of whitewashing in their teaching of history (children's religious textbooks were the worst). It was as slanted as the revolutionary histories I had read.

A lot of it was moving but funny. There was, for example, a spiritual version of the rags to riches theme in many of them, but as for many religious people spiritual riches mean rags, the result is confusing. The happy ending comes when the person concerned finds God in a leper colony or in a sewer. The amusement fades when one realizes it is true. On her way to concentration camp, Edith Stein wrote that she was "praying wonderfully". When I read it, I stopped smiling.

There is another type about which I feel fewer inhibitions. These biographies seem very like Angela Brazil schoolgirl stories as retold by Arthur Marshall. There is a racy excitement about them and I skip pages to find out what happened next. The hero or heroine is hooked on heroin and assaulted by inner lusts and external lechers until he or she meets up with brand X evangelism or a Rabbi or nun with a guitar: you can write the ending for yourself. As in the story of Edith Stein, the difficulty is that a lot of these histories are true. It may be peculiar, but it is not always synthetic or pop, and in religion you have to get used to the peculiar – inspired silences, kabbalistic sparks, domestic miracles from India, public miracles at Fatima, spinning dervishes, cures at Lourdes and speaking in tongues. One does not know what to make of it all, but the world is a more interesting place. Under materialist régimes of whatever type it gets a bit dull. Everyone, rich and destitute alike, enjoys his bit of opium. People cannot do without it in fact, as party leaders have found out to their sorrow and disgust.

I turned more and more to the classics of mysticism. They were the easiest religious books to read, which impressed me. In my own religion law was the daily bread of religious study and mysticism only came when you were advanced in years and virtue with a teacher even older and more advanced than you. The subjects had changed places. The mystical writings were now daily bread, while the details of law were fascinating but exotic. I think this reversal affected many young Jews I know, and not only Jews but Christians and others as well. The greatest mystical treatise of medieval England, *The Cloud of Unknowing*, was written for an austere contemplative, and other readers are carefully warned off. It is now a best-seller and lies next to the detective stories in station bookshops. One can be sure that its readers are not that austere or contemplative. It satisfies a need which is deep but popular and contemporary.

A Marxist friend caught me reading this forbidden literature and I had a lot of explaining to do, both to him and myself. The mystical classics are deficient in sociology and historical awareness. At least their authors have neither more nor less than anyone else in their time. This means that you have to swallow hard at first when you read them. In the Buber version of Chassidic stories, the mystics and Rabbis seem to have no awareness of the role they played unwittingly in Russian politics and the changing economic structure of the Jewish world about them. In a similar way, Teresa of Avila tries to make reparation for the Reformation with her life. As she never understood its social and economic causes, could she understand what she was making reparation for? One cannot blame her for not anticipating Max Weber or Tawney, but it does mean that a modern person has to supply a missing dimension.

Although they are closer in time than the Scriptures, these books too require a lot of inner translation and commentary before they can be used. A student I know showed me the Tanya of the Lubavitch Chassidim. It made religious sense, but you have to be prepared to swallow the medieval cosmology it assumes. Thérèse of Lisieux needs similar treatment. If you strip away the antimacassars, the "little flowers" and the gore, you find something ruthless and relevant to your own life. The late nineteenth-century packaging in which her message comes is offputting, and you have to overcome your prejudices to get at the genuine goods she has to offer.

As I have said, fewer people live at the centre of their own religion today. For many the tradition is a compass point which helps one chart one's own position. One does not have to stand directly on it. People are also religiously on the move. They usually end up where they started, but their journey takes them through many forms of belief and doubt. As a result the old No-man's-land between the traditional systems is now becoming heavily populated with religious seekers. In fact it is getting much more difficult to find anyone who is a wholehearted inhabitant of the old fortresses, jealously patrolling the fence round tradition. No-man's-land too has its saints, its mystics and its teachers. They are probably the easiest to understand for religious pilgrims today. Being outside a formal discipline, they are more wayward, but their faults can be seen more clearly because there is less gloss over them and less fulsome propaganda around them. Martin Buber did not attend synagogue, and he is still not *persona grata* with Jewish religious or secular authorities. He was, for example, not allowed to teach religion at the Hebrew University in Jerusalem, only sociology. Nevertheless he has been the religious teacher and Pied Piper of two or three generations of Jews, Christians and outsiders.

When I first read Simone Weil, another inhabitant of No-man's-land, her Jewish anti-Judaism irritated me beyond endurance. Everything good came from the Greeks, everything bad from the Hebrews. Her view of the Bible (Old Testament) was one sided, fascinating, and at times absurd. She must have irritated Catholics as much as she irritated Jews. Though she seemed to believe in her own way, she refused to get baptized and ended up as a sort of Christian who had consciously decided to stand outside the Church. Later on I read her Notebooks. Like most great religious figures, there was a ruthless logical quality in her writing which rang true. On trains and planes, I could not help underlining sentences and wanting to throw the book away. She taught me a lot, as did all the other outsiders, Kafka, Tolstoy, Edward Carpenter and Vivekananda, the first Hindu apostle to the West. They are an odd bunch, but reading them it seems that there was more real religious thinking outside the systems than inside them. They are good teachers for those who do not want to join anything but wish spiritually to go it alone.

Like many people, I wanted at first to find one system or one guru who had the answers to all my problems. I met quite a few who had the answers, but they were the wrong ones. Reluctantly I decided that such a creature was not to be found. Reality was too complex to fit one system or one person. Each of us had a part of the answer, and out of the fragments I had to construct my own composite guru. There are a lot of cracks, and I prefer them to show. I do not trust people who "know" too much and have more awareness of God than they have of their own limitations.

I constructed my composite guru, as I have said, while thumbing through paperbacks at airports or sitting in a train careering through Europe at night. My theology, such as it is, was worked out on the move. It is quite appropriate, for I have always felt a visitor in the world – it is my habitation but not my home.

Chapter Twenty-three

The consolations of religion

A rabbi fell asleep and dreamt that he had entered Paradise.
There, to his surprise, he found sages discussing a knotty
problem in the Talmud.

"Is this the reward of Paradise?" cried the rabbi. "Why,
they did the very same thing on earth!"

At this he heard a voice chiding him: "You foolish man!
You think the sages are in Paradise. It's just the opposite!
Paradise is in the sages."

A Treasury of Jewish Folklore

My soul, there is a country
   far beyond the stars
Where stands a winged sentry
   all skilfull in the wars . . .
If thou canst get but thither
   there grows the flower of peace
The rose that cannot wither
   thy fortress and thy ease.

Henry Vaughan

I have tried to give an account of how religion actually came to
me, not an account of the final product. For in truth there is
no final product. My faith is still on the move, and the
formulations, the theologies and the language it uses are
always expanding and contracting like amoebae as new
experience is sensed and absorbed. I have tried to describe

the nucleus of experience which does not change. This nucleus formed itself long ago in my childhood years and its possibilities and limitations were fairly clear to me when I became a Rabbi. I have therefore concentrated on these years with their spots, pimples and clumsiness, for they were the years of perception, not the years of rationalization.

Whenever I have met other believers, I have always wanted to go behind the finished product, the rationale of their faith, to the primitive "how" and "why" of it all. The toughness of early sketches tells me more than the varnished surface of the final painting. When I handle a religious cheque, I want to know what experience there is in the bank to back it. I have not tried for myself to give the one answer, but just the clumsy working out of my own religious answer. This kind of testimony is now of greater importance, because surface smoothness can be got too easily and evokes no trust. I hope other priests, ministers and Rabbis will risk telling their stories too, especially the early parts, the adolescent parts, the clumsy parts. Much religion has crumbled, a few of these stories might still be useful in a time of change.

But time has not changed certain problems. In one sense God is no nearer now than He ever was. One progresses in religion but the horizon is no closer. What has changed is that it doesn't seem to matter so much. I have more religious responsibilities now, but I seem to cover more ground on less spiritual fuel. Another problem which remains unchanged is forgiveness. The rituals do not seem to touch it. I am welded to my past with its sins and silliness. I can't get rid of it, and it can't get rid of me. So we will have to learn to live together, die together and proceed to judgement together. What has changed is that I rely more on the obvious, on my own hunch. Sin is what feels like sin, not what ought to be sin. I can spot it at least, though I cannot make it vanish as a conjurer can with a rabbit. I have needed spirituality to be straightforward. I can sometimes pray simply now, without trite "thee-thouism" or embarrassing over-familiarities. This seemed very new until I read some passages on sin, forgiveness and prayer, whose truth I recognized, and found that the author was Calvin!

The "consolations of religion" have not changed that much either, but they have grown up like me. I like the phrase "consolations of religion". I found it in one of those pious magazines. The author seemed to know exactly what they were and so presumably did his readers because he never spelt them out. So I had to spell them out for myself, as concretely as I could, as the Consoler is of course invisible, which is a nuisance but necessary it seems.

I do not think there is much mystery about them. They may be personal but they are not unique, and they are available to anybody who, for example, takes the trouble to go into an empty church or synagogue and keep an hour's silence. The awareness which comes has been attested time and time again in the history of Judaism and every other faith I have known. It has not only been experienced by Rabbis and mystics, but by navvies and housewives as well, and all religion is based on it. Some people say, "Only an occasional hour – nothing more?" For most people this is quite enough as a start, but it is surprising how few people can stick it, despite all the reassurance that there is a light at the other end and that the only risk is boredom.

People think they have to do more than they need, and get discouraged. If there is any reality in it all, it means that you are not the only one involved. You may be searching for God, but this would not help you if He were not searching for you, for the distance is immense, beyond the intellect and the imagination. A hand comes down from heaven, so to speak. Prayer makes us ready to grasp it and trust its strength.

One of the consolations of religion is precisely this – that we are not alone. I found it inconvenient, this other voice inside me, separate from my own, and it gave my conduct an erratic quality. Gradually over the years the two have learnt to live together. Occasionally the two voices even fuse, and this is a great bliss though a rare one. But since I accepted it, I have never felt alone.

This awareness seems very slight, but what it can take is amazing. I do not know how "real" my experience has been. As I have said, I do not know if the childhood meeting "really" took place, though I think it did. I can describe, but I cannot account for the later meetings. All of it seems transparent, almost nothing in fact. Yet when I lean upon this nothing, it supports me, and when I look into it, it looks into me and I see myself naked – really naked, not just without clothes. Once again this individual experience is also a communal one. Because Judaism trusted in the unseen and what was not there, it survived. Those who trusted in something more real have not.

Another "consolation" is its practical value. If I had not trusted those signs, those hints of a greater reality, I would certainly have ceased to grow. I would have shrivelled. They have been and still are my only protection against being hijacked by society or my own ego. I have seen good people who did not follow their own signs and became reflections of the media or of success. They began to lose their souls, and I did not want it to happen to me.

I use this awareness as a touchstone. I hold things up to it: my feelings, my ambitions and my phantasies. It illuminates them, and I know what I must put aside and what I can keep. I rarely want to thank it – most liturgy I think overdoes this – it needs to be used not complimented. The only things I ask of it with reasonable confidence are the knowledge of what I should do next or the perception of what is really going on – in me and around me. I suppose if I had greater trust I should ask more, but modesty and common sense restrain me. I cannot ask more than I believe.

I should like to stress that with the awareness of God, the world does not vanish, it is the same world as before, the world which is seen by everyone. Nevertheless in the light of this awareness, a transformation does take place. Things which seemed important fade into shadows and insignificance. Dark areas light up, and incidents which were small or rejected begin to glow – and become the land-marks in my life. It redefines success and failure, triumph and tragedy. With it I am released from the pull of my conditioning and can for a moment see clearly without the distortions of hope or fear. It gives me courage to think my own thoughts, not packaged ones, and to walk one step alone, if I have to.

I can do this more easily, because the steps lead me home. I have come to understand what this haunting word means for me. It is not any of the houses I have lived in. It is the reality I have come from, the reality I go to – and the reality that is woven into my life. I have doubts about messianism and whether time will alter anything. The reality is as real now as it will ever be. I am open to it now or never. There is no reason why the situation should change.

Occasionally, when I have conducted a funeral or cremation, I have felt that a part of myself was moving forward with the coffin. It was not frightening, because I realized that a part of me was already invested in what one calls life beyond death. It is that part of me which is in a position to judge myself with some detachment and which can begin to see the world without illusions, less distorted by hope or fear.

This presence I have talked about has followed me wherever I have trotted, and I think it will follow me across that frontier too; whatever "I" shall be, "I" shall need its company, because the laws of causation will not cease with the death of my body.

Some "consolations of religion" are not very consoling. Religion is misrepresented as insurance which it is not. It is more like a launching pad into the unknown. As a minister of religion, I ought not to sell security but courage. (I try, but I cannot always pass on what I have not got.)

There is no direct relationship between religion and straightforward happiness. Look at religious lives! One is forbidden to enter the promised land, another dies on a cross and another dies early of consumption or in a concentration camp. Even if such people are left alone, they can starve themselves into holy anorexia. But beyond happiness there are other experiences – joy, contentment and grace. They may seem thin, like being served ambrosia when you want rare roast beef, but they are real too. They are more real for example than the bright happiness of a cocktail party or the smiles at a business lunch.

Because of this faulty connection with happiness, it is wise to consider what prayer involves. If you ask, you might have to receive. It might be better if you had never asked. There has to be a letting-go, a giving-up in the will, and this certainly seems frightening.

Against all these cautions is the adventure of religion, and the exhilaration of it. When you can see, you do not want to return to the dark, though the world is not a pretty place. It is one of the rare forms of awareness which make you grow up towards it, and which does not cut "it" down to your size.

Like Nicholas of Cusa, it is summed up for me in an image. It is early morning, and I am on a small boat in northern Holland. We pass under the shadow of the watergate at Sneek. Behind me is the waking town, ahead of me the land falls away, and there is endless water, great clouds and streaming light. I feel freedom, and exultation and wonder. For some, religion means coming into harbour – for me it is adventure with a companion and a shining vista.

Chapter Twenty-four

Penny plain
or tuppence coloured?

One hour of repentance and good deeds in this world is
better than all the life of the world to come; and one hour of
calmness of spirit in the world to come is better
than all the life of this world.

Sayings of the Fathers

"What is Thy servant but a dog!"

Ancient Semitic Inscription

The lines which end the last chapter sound very romantic,
rather like a second-feature movie, but the problem with
religion is not romantic, just crude and simple, and I did not
learn it from any guru whom I had to chase up in some
inconvenient cave in the Himalayas, but right at home, from
my dog Re'ach. Readers of the Bible should not be surprised
by this animal intrusion, because though dogs and horses get
a bad press there (eating up Jezebel, obstinacy and lust),
animals make good prophets as well as pets.

Indeed the opening lines of the Hebrew liturgy at Jewish
services were not first spoken by a Jew, but by Balaam the
Jew-hater, and even more surprisingly, his mentor was an ass.
The word of God is mediated to us through many
messengers. It is only our snobbism which prevents us re-
ceiving it. I learnt a lot about religion from my dog Re'ach.
You always do from any being you love.

This was how I learnt it. Whenever I left my house, my dog Re'ach would look at me mournfully and reproachfully from the stairs – the tragic look on her face reminded me of Bette Davis, registering sorrow and passion in *Now Voyager*, a film which had moved me profoundly in my youth. Re'ach was a very Jewish dog. No wonder dogs were not favoured by the prophets, they were so much better at inducing guilt.

Whenever I came back the reverse would take place. As I opened the door, Re'ach turned, amazed, towards it. Now dogs can't laugh but they can show astonishment. Re'ach being a Jewish dog showed it in a big way. She leapt down the stairs, woofing and baying, and then brought me down in an amorous tackle. Standing on my chest she would lick me triumphantly and ecstatically, like a canine Orpheus whose Euridice was on reprieve.

This drama took place whether I had been on a long visit to North America or on a short errand to the newspaper man round the corner. Eventually wearying of this dramatic life, I went to consult my vet. "Doesn't she learn from experience?" I complained. "Is she so dumb that she never realizes I'll come back, or does she like emotional orgies?"

Patiently he explained my dog to me. "Being an animal," he said, "and very attached to you, she can't help these great disturbances." "You see," he added, "people and things are real for her when they are within the range of her senses. When she can see you, touch you, smell you (smelling is the most important), you are alive. When you move outside the range of her senses, it is as if you were dead. Now you can understand her a bit better. How would you feel if someone you loved died and was resurrected every weekend and twice on most weekdays?" I paused to consider my life under such circumstances and agreed weakly that it would certainly be rocky.

Now, according to the psalms we are a little higher than animals, and just a little lower than the angels. No wonder religion is tough in such an inbetween situation. Because we are a little lower than the angels we are able to accept the reality of a being and a world we can't sense – but only just! The kingdom of heaven is not a foreign country to us and we know it is not fairyland. But our hold on it is very weak, because we are only a little higher than the animals, not very far from my poor dog Re'ach. In fact we humans have the same difficulty of ascribing life to a *mysterium tremendum*, as she has in ascribing it to me when I am absent. Like her, what is not sensed quickly becomes nonsense for us.

When we deal with spiritual matters, we are working at the limit of our perception – finite animals reaching out to infinity.

I think it is more difficult for me to hold on to the intangible now than it was when I first dropped into that Quaker meeting so many years ago at Oxford. Advertising has got slicker and there is more of it. It has persuaded me that I need a lot more things – not that I needed much persuading. In the early fifties, for example, men were only permitted a slick of brilliantine. Deodorants were finickety, and bath salts pansy. We must have smelt rather gamey, like venison, but we were not aware of it. Now I pack my pre-shave, after-shave and splash-on, even when I am off to an ascetic retreat.

Like most people, I have got happiness and comfort well and truly muddled. Each year I look through the tourist brochures, and buy myself a chunk of escapism on a Costa because the pictures assure me (though the print is reticent) that happiness will come too, as a bonus extra, like those old trading stamps we used to get handed to us. (They looked so grand and were worth so little.) And yet I know that it never works out like that. Happiness, like the kingdom of heaven, is within me. Yes, I would prefer to be unhappy in comfort than in discomfort, but I have been very happy in a boarding house, and suicidal in a de-luxe hotel. Comfort means objects, but happiness is of the spirit. It's a truth so easy to state and so difficult to live.

This sounds so spiritual that I suspect it. It slips down too easily, like cheap romances. Being an inbetween person I have to do justice to both the realities in which I live and have my being. Spirituality can be trusted only if it can deal sanely, sensibly and helpfully with its twin, the material world. It's no use loving people's souls if you are disgusted by their liver and lights. The material world is the testing ground of all spirituality.

A lot of it fails the test. A lot of spirituality (especially, for some reason, if it is in French) sounds very inspiring. But then as you are reading it on the top of a crowded bus you can't help asking yourself, "Now what did all that mean?" And a dreadful suspicion forms in your mind. "Did it mean anything at all?"

I don't think we can be sure, unless our spirituality is accompanied by an attestation from the material world. I have never ceased to brood over the strange portion of the Pentateuch I had to read at my confirmation – my Bar Mitzvah, at which I "became a man". On thinking it over, the guts and gore of the sacrifices came from my ancestors' possessions and they didn't have many, only their animals. When these went up in smoke on the altar, so did their shares and Building Society accounts and pension funds. The guts were crude, but they made their sin offerings and guilt offerings real, and validated them.

I sat in a reserved seat in a crowded train. I had reserved it because I needed to read a book on spirituality. It was hot stuff, and as I read it God seemed to come very close to me. So did a noisy lady standing in the gangway. The book seemed to tell me quite clearly that the reality of God is more important than any experience of Him. Reluctantly obedient, and thoroughly annoyed, I closed the book and gave up my seat. It was my sacrifice. Unless I had made it, I could never have opened that book again.

The experience of God came a lot at the start of my dive into religion, and I hope I will get a dollop of it at the end to ease my entry into eternity. But in the meantime I have had to make do with the reality of God. (It's not always God I've prayed for, but success or ease or evasion which I've dressed up in divinity. No wonder such prayers were never answered.)

Some friendships of many years were coming to an end. Before, we had all helped each other, now it didn't work out like that. There was the usual froth of self-justification which marks all changes in direction, with their accompanying insecurities (I said.... you said ..... he said ...... she said ......), the whining, the trivial points of honour, the secret scoreboard of hidden hurts. As the instincts launched me into this tedious and selfish exercise, I prayed ... not to get my way, or to score, or even to patch things up, but to give up with affection and if possible with love. And the presence of God seemed to move into the faces of my friends, and well ... we still speak occasionally and we may help each other again though in a different way, God willing. That's all, and that's religion ... when you face a blank wall, faith is knowing that there is a door, if it is a door you want and pray for. The experience of St John of the Cross is relevant in a suburban parlour.

This "failure" concealed a "success" which concealed a hidden danger. To cheer myself up in the empty evenings which followed, coming home to a room in which the washing up I left in the morning remained exactly as I had left it, I called on God to enlighten me. He preferred to lighten me instead. As I have said before, I had always expected religion to make me heavy, but in fact it gave me back once again both love and laughter, as it had done in the Quaker meeting house in Oxford.

Jokes and humour burst into my prayers. I dispensed this mixture over the radio, and found it had the same effect on others as it had on me. To my astonishment, I became a celebrity (third class, after Arthur Scargill and Norman Tebbit). I never thought the rewards of the Spirit would be like this, and decided to take another look at the last verses of Job, and their suburban happy ending – the ones that many spiritual people get snooty about.

Although spirituality is see-through, without it the real world goes wrong very easily. If you are over-preoccupied with sex, you can become very trivial; if you are mastered by your "image", you become phony to yourself. My own experience has taught me that the pieties of religion are not commands but functional necessities of life – not cake but bread, ordinary bread – absolutely necessary for my self-respect.

It pleases me that God has become ordinary to me. He (or She – I have to learn to adjust) is no longer an exotic experience, bedecked with the tinsel jewellery of the imagination. In fact I don't get worried if I don't experience Him at all. For the reality of God makes the experience of Him a toy. This reality is enough with its silences, its doubts, and the busy business of religion. God is as much in them as He was in the previous technicolour episodes, but I have to learn what is being said to me through the obvious.

For what is this reality which endures when the imagination gets tired and goes to sleep? It is being nice to other people, trying to love them and if you can't at least not hating them, passing plates at parties, helping them with their luggage, telling them the time without making a fuss, letting yourself be used without becoming a door mat, and keeping your integrity in a tricky time.

Now I hear you say, "Rabbi Blue, what dull stuff! Why, it's the kind of thing people teach in any old-fashioned Sunday School." And I answer a bit ruefully, "Yes, you're right, it is. The only difference is that once I tried to teach it to children, now as an adult I try to learn it myself." It seems an awfully long journey to rediscover my own platitudes. But at last I know their heights and depths.

And I can hear Him cackling His head off!

Epilogue

Some years ago in *To Heaven with Scribes and Pharisees* I tried to describe the working faith of a community – my own. In this book I have tried to describe the working faith of a single member of it – my own. It is not meant for Sunday School use nor for confirmation classes. Not all adult religion and experience can be contained in such a setting, nor indeed should it be. It is meant for adults then – some of them – who may be helped to identify their own experience. Some parts of it may seem bizarre, for the actual experience of any individual remains individual, though it can be shared. I have not tried to describe a system of theology, but the story of a seed of faith which became rooted in my mind, and the way it grew. This growth would not have been possible without my community, which gave me a religious home, and the time and freedom to find my own place in it.

Also available in Fount Paperbacks

BOOKS BY DAVID KOSSOFF

Bible Stories

'To my mind there is no doubt that these stories make the Bible
come alive. Mr Kossoff is a born storyteller. He has the gift of
making the old stories new.'

William Barclay

The Book of Witnesses

'The little stories are fascinating in the warm humanity they
reveal. Right from the first one the reader is enthralled . . .
bringing the drama of the New Testament into our daily lives with
truly shattering impact.'

Religious Book News

The Voices of Masada

'This is imaginative historical writing of the highest standard.'

Church Times

The Little Book of Sylvanus

Sylvanus, the quiet, observant man, tells his version of the events
surrounding the 'carpenter preacher' of Nazareth, from the
Crucifixion to Pentecost. A moving and unforgettable view of the
gospel story, and a sequel to *The Book of Witnesses*.

Fount Paperbacks

Fount is one of the leading paperback publishers of religious books and below are some of its recent titles.

- ☐ THE QUIET HEART George Appleton £2.95
- ☐ PRAYER FOR ALL TIMES Pierre Charles £1.75
- ☐ SEEKING GOD Esther de Waal £1.75
- ☐ THE SCARLET AND THE BLACK
  J. P. Gallagher £1.75
- ☐ TELL MY PEOPLE I LOVE THEM
  Clifford Hill £1.50
- ☐ CONVERSATIONS WITH THE CRUCIFIED
  Reid Isaac £1.50
- ☐ THE LITTLE BOOK OF SYLVANUS
  David Kossoff £1.50
- ☐ DOES GOD EXIST? Hans Küng £5.95
- ☐ GEORGE MACDONALD: AN ANTHOLOGY
  George MacDonald C. S. Lewis (ed.) £1.50
- ☐ WHY I AM STILL A CATHOLIC
  Robert Nowell (ed.) £1.50
- ☐ THE GOSPEL FROM OUTER SPACE
  Robert L. Short £1.50
- ☐ CONTINUALLY AWARE Rita Snowden £1.75
- ☐ TRUE RESURRECTION Harry Williams £1.75
- ☐ WHO WILL DELIVER US? Paul Zahl £1.50

All Fount paperbacks are available at your bookshop or newsagent, or they can also be ordered by post from Fount Paperbacks, Cash Sales Department, G.P.O. Box 29, Douglas, Isle of Man, British Isles. Please send purchase price, plus 15p per book, maximum postage £3. Customers outside the U.K. send purchase price, plus 15p per book. Cheque, postal or money order. No currency.

NAME (Block letters) _____

ADDRESS _____

_____

_____